Current CONTROVERSIES

Domestic Wiretapping

Other Books in the Current Controversies Series

Domestic Wiretapping

Sylvia Engdahl, Book Editor

GREENHAVEN PRESS
A part of Gale, Cengage Learning

GALE
CENGAGE Learning™

Detroit • New York • San Francisco • New Haven, Conn • Waterville, Maine • London

Christine Nasso, *Publisher*
Elizabeth Des Chenes, *Managing Editor*

© 2008 Greenhaven Press, a part of Gale, Cengage Learning

Gale and Greenhaven Press are registered trademarks used herein under license.

For more information, contact:
Greenhaven Press
27500 Drake Rd.
Farmington Hills, MI 48331-3535
Or you can visit our Internet site at gale.cengage.com

For product information and technology assistance, contact us at

Gale Customer Support, 1-800-877-4253
For permission to use material from this text or product, submit all requests online at
www.cengage.com/permissions

Further permissions questions can be emailed to permissionrequest@cengage.com

Articles in Greenhaven Press anthologies are often edited for length to meet page require-ments. In addition, original titles of these works are changed to clearly present the main thesis and to explicitly indicate the author's opinion. Every effort is made to ensure that Greenhaven Press accurately reflects the original intent of the authors. Every effort has been made to trace the owners of copyrighted material.

Cover image copyright Marcin Balcerzak, 2007. Used under license of Shutterstock.com.

LIBRARY OF CONGRESS CATALOGING-IN-PUBLICATION DATA

Domestic wiretapping / Sylvia Engdahl, book editor.
    p. cm. -- (Current controversies)
    Includes bibliographical references and index.
    ISBN-13: 978-0-7377-3958-9 (hardcover)
    ISBN-13: 978-0-7377-3959-6 (pbk.)
    1. Wiretapping--United States--Juvenile literature. I. Engdahl, Sylvia.
    KF9670.D66 2008
    345.73'052--dc22

                                2008001006

Printed in the United States of America
1 2 3 4 5   12 11 10 09 08

Contents

Chapter 3: Should the Foreign Intelligence Surveillance Act (FISA) Be Modernized?

Yes: The FISA Must Be Updated to Deal with International Terrorism

Chapter 4: How Are New Technologies Affecting Domestic Wiretapping?

Foreword

By definition, controversies are "discussions of questions in which opposing opinions clash" (Webster's Twentieth Century Dictionary Unabridged). Few would deny that controversies are a pervasive part of the human condition and exist on virtually every level of human enterprise. Controversies transpire between individuals and among groups, within nations and between nations. Controversies supply the grist necessary for progress by providing challenges and challengers to the status quo. They also create atmospheres where strife and warfare can flourish. A world without controversies would be a peaceful world; but it also would be, by and large, static and prosaic.

The Series' Purpose

The purpose of the *Current Controversies* series is to explore many of the social, political, and economic controversies dominating the national and international scenes today. Titles selected for inclusion in the series are highly focused and specific. For example, from the larger category of criminal justice, *Current Controversies* deals with specific topics such as police brutality, gun control, white collar crime, and others. The debates in *Current Controversies* also are presented in a useful, timeless fashion. Articles and book excerpts included in each title are selected if they contribute valuable, long-range ideas to the overall debate. And wherever possible, current information is enhanced with historical documents and other relevant materials. Thus, while individual titles are current in focus, every effort is made to ensure that they will not become quickly outdated. Books in the *Current Controversies* series will remain important resources for librarians, teachers, and students for many years.

In addition to keeping the titles focused and specific, great care is taken in the editorial format of each book in the series. Book introductions and chapter prefaces are offered to provide background material for readers. Chapters are organized around several key questions that are answered with diverse opinions representing all points on the political spectrum. Materials in each chapter include opinions in which authors clearly disagree as well as alternative opinions in which authors may agree on a broader issue but disagree on the possible solutions. In this way, the content of each volume in *Current Controversies* mirrors the mosaic of opinions encountered in society. Readers will quickly realize that there are many viable answers to these complex issues. By questioning each author's conclusions, students and casual readers can begin to develop the critical thinking skills so important to evaluating opinionated material.

Current Controversies is also ideal for controlled research. Each anthology in the series is composed of primary sources taken from a wide gamut of informational categories including periodicals, newspapers, books, U.S. and foreign government documents, and the publications of private and public organizations. Readers will find factual support for reports, debates, and research papers covering all areas of important issues. In addition, an annotated table of contents, an index, a book and periodical bibliography, and a list of organizations to contact are included in each book to expedite further research.

Perhaps more than ever before in history, people are confronted with diverse and contradictory information. During the Persian Gulf War, for example, the public was not only treated to minute-to-minute coverage of the war, it was also inundated with critiques of the coverage and countless analyses of the factors motivating U.S. involvement. Being able to sort through the plethora of opinions accompanying today's major issues, and to draw one's own conclusions, can be a complicated and frustrating struggle. It is the editors' hope that *Current Controversies* will help readers with this struggle.

Introduction

Wiretapping and related forms of electronic surveillance are common tools used by law enforcement agencies to catch and convict criminals. Most people agree that this method is good as long as the constitutional rights of the targeted suspects are preserved. However, after the terrorist attacks of September 11, 2001, it seemed necessary to watch suspected terrorists as well. In the past, it was assumed that there were not many active enemies of the United States operating within its borders; U.S. intelligence agencies spied on them outside the United States but were not allowed to do any domestic spying. September 11 changed that, for Congress soon passed the PATRIOT Act, thus permitting the wiretapping procedures previously used only against criminals to also be used against suspected terrorists.

The Patriot Act was controversial. Some people felt that the constitutional rights of Americans were no longer being sufficiently protected. Because of this criticism, many provisions of the act were set to expire after four years. Therefore, they were reconsidered by Congress in 2005. While the debate was going on, the news media revealed that a secret domestic spying program was being conducted by the National Security Agency (NSA) to investigate suspected terrorists—a program under which the rules of the Foreign Intelligence Surveillance Act (FISA) were not being observed. According to the FISA, domestic wiretapping cannot be used without a warrant, although the procedure for obtaining warrants is less restrictive than that for getting warrants in criminal investigations. The NSA surveillance, which was carried out under an executive order of President George W. Bush, failed to follow that procedure and is therefore commonly called the "warrantless wiretapping program."

A public debate arose over the question of whether the president's authorization of this program was illegal. Eventually, the president agreed to conform to the FISA. However, he and his supporters insisted that the FISA was not adequate to deal with terrorism and needed to be modernized. In August of 2007 Congress amended it by passing the Protect America Act, which allows the government to eavesdrop on domestic communications without court permission as long as one end of the conversation is "reasonably believed" to be outside the United States. But that act was intended to be temporary; it was to be reconsidered after six months. By the time this book reaches libraries, a new law will have been passed, but whatever its provisions may be, not everyone will agree with them. It is unlikely that Americans will reach consensus on these issues.

The controversy centers on the degree to which the Constitution protects the privacy of American citizens. Many people feel that for the government to have access to innocent citizens' phone calls and e-mails is a serious invasion of privacy, even if officials do not actually examine any except those suspected of involving terrorism or crime. Others believe that the need to investigate potential terrorists—whose identity may not be known in advance—justifies collecting domestic data and that doing so does no harm to anyone who has nothing to hide.

Donald Kerr, the principal deputy director of National Intelligence, suggested in an October 2007 speech that privacy should be redefined. It should no longer be equated with anonymity because "in our interconnected and wireless world . . . anonymity is quickly becoming a thing of the past." When so much data is collected and available on MySpace and Facebook and YouTube, he said, "Protecting anonymity isn't a fight that can be won. Anybody that's typed in their name on Google understands that. Instead, privacy is a system of laws, rules and customs . . . on which our intelligence community commitment is based and measured. And it is that framework that we need to grow and nourish and adjust as our cultures change."

Kerr went on to say he thought it was strange that people let unscreened employees of credit card companies and Internet service providers handle their personal data yet were unwilling to let government employees do so, considering that it is a felony punishable by jail and a large fine for the latter to misuse such data. Bloggers were quick to point out that not everyone chooses to reveal personal information on the Internet and that in any case, just because people voluntarily give out information does not mean they want the government to collect it from other sources without their consent. Nor, some believe, can the government be trusted to define "misuse."

One contentious issue being debated by Congress is whether telecom companies that helped the NSA in its surveillance of domestic communications should be immune from being sued for breach of contract with their customers. So far about forty such suits have been filed in an effort to get the program reviewed by federal courts and ruled illegal. Those who support these suits say it will not be possible to fully investigate the government's surveillance activities if those who participated are immune from testifying in court and that the companies should not be allowed to get away with breaking the law. But others argue that private companies should not be held responsible for what the government does, both because it would be unfair to expect them to refuse official requests and because if the spying was not legal, then the government ought to take full blame. The president and intelligence authorities maintain that allowing the suits to go forward would require public release of information that would aid terrorists and compromise national security.

Opposition to the granting of retroactive immunity to telecom companies increased after former AT&T technician Mark Klein revealed that the NSA had built a secret room at the facility where he worked and had been copying all the traffic that came across the Internet cables, domestic as well as foreign. "It struck me at the time," he said in a November 2007 interview posted on YouTube, "that this is a massively unconstitutional, illegal operation."

Congress appeared unwilling let the telecom companies off the hook. Many members favored amendments to the FISA that did not give these companies blanket amnesty, and would thus permit the pending lawsuits against them to proceed. After President Bush said that he would veto such a bill, a tentative agreement was reached, and on February 12, 2008 the Senate passed, by an overwhelming majority, a bill that does grant immunity to the telecom companies. But the House of Representatives declined to vote on it before adjourning for a recess, and so on February 18 the Protect America Act was allowed to expire.

As of March 1, 2008 the controversy continues. "If what [the telecom companies] did was not wrong, then what fear should they have of litigation?" said an editorial in the *Arizona Wildcat*, expressing an opinion widely held by opponents of the bill. "Immunity will only beget ignorance and secrecy—an enemy far more dangerous than any terrorist."

Supporters of the bill, on the other hand, believe that much of the opposition in the House is the result of lobbying by lawyers eager to pursue the pending lawsuits and that failure to renew the Protect America Act seriously compromises national security. The *New York Post* declared, "Let's be clear: The law's expiration will seriously hamper the ability of U.S. intelligence agencies to monitor communications of America's enemies." President Bush agreed. At news conference he stated, "Protecting these companies from lawsuits is not a partisan issue. . . . Republicans and Democrats in the House stand ready to pass the Senate bill, if House leaders would only stop blocking an up or down vote and let the majority in the House prevail."

CHAPTER 1

Are the Wiretapping Provisions of the Patriot Act Necessary?

Chapter Preface

The Uniting and Strengthening America by Providing Appropriate Tools Required to Intercept and Obstruct Terrorism Act of 2001, which is known (from the initial letters of the words in its title) as the USA PATRIOT Act or just the Patriot Act, was passed by wide margins in Congress shortly after the terrorist attacks of September 11, 2001. Nearly everyone agreed that measures to prevent more terrorist attacks were needed. However, some people felt that the Patriot Act went too far, that it encroached on the civil liberties of law-abiding Americans. For this reason, Congress decided that it should be reconsidered after approximately four years and set many of its provisions to expire, or "sunset," on December 31, 2005. The viewpoints in this chapter are from the 2005 debate over its renewal.

Electronic surveillance—generally called "wiretapping" although with modern technology such surveillance rarely involves actual tapping of wires—is only one of the activities with which the Patriot Act deals. The authorization of governmental access to library records is even more controversial, and there are some provisions that have not been challenged. This book covers only those related to wiretapping that were scheduled to expire. These include the following:

- Section 201: Gives the government authority to intercept wire, oral, and electronic communications relating to terrorism.

- Section 202: Gives the government authority to intercept wire, oral, and electronic communications relating to computer fraud and abuse.

- Section 203(b) and (d): Allows information to be shared between law enforcement officials and intelligence agencies.

- Section 204: Removes limits on wiretapping U.S. persons if the information is gathered outside the United States.

- Section 206: Allows wiretapping ("roving wiretaps") under a single order of all communications used by a target of investigation, instead of just one particular phone.

- Section 207: Allows the investigation of a suspect under the Foreign Intelligence Surveillance Act (FISA) to continue for a longer period of time than in the past.

- Section 209: Makes the procedure for authorizing investigators' access to voice mail the same as for e-mail.

- Section 212: Authorizes providers of communications services to disclose the content or records of subscribers' communications without delay in emergencies involving immediate danger of death or serious injury.

- Section 214: Allows investigators to access records of all calls to and from a phone, excluding the content of the calls, using pen registers (for outgoing calls) and trap-and-trace devices (for incoming calls).

- Section 217: Allows computer service providers who are victims of hacking to let law enforcement officials monitor the trespassers, regardless of privacy laws.

- Section 218: Lowers the standard of evidence for FISA warrants.

- Section 220: Allows courts to issue search warrants that apply anywhere in the United States instead of just in their own districts.

- Section 223: Allows investigators who break the rules for electronic surveillance to be sued.

- Section 225: Gives immunity against being sued to phone companies, Internet service providers, and others who assist intelligence agencies in wiretapping under the FISA.

As is evident in the following viewpoints, there were sharp differences of opinion about many of these provisions. The debate went on for months, and the date for expiration was extended several times. Finally, on March 7, 2006, Congress authorized renewal of the Patriot Act, with some modifications to safeguard civil liberties, and two days later it was signed into law by the president. The roving wiretap authorization was set to expire in 2010 unless renewed again; all the others related to wiretapping were to be permanent.

Investigators Need to Use the Same Tools Against Terrorists as Against Other Criminals

George W. Bush

George W. Bush was the forty-third president of the United States. The son of former United States president George H. W. Bush, he was first inaugurated in January, 2001. Previously, he served as governor of Texas. The following viewpoint is a speech he gave at the Ohio State Police Academy.

My most solemn duty as President is to protect the American people. And I'm honored to share that responsibility with you. We have a joint responsibility. As sworn officers of the law, you're devoted to defending your fellow citizens. Your vigilance is keeping our communities safe, and you're serving on the front lines of the war on terror. It's a different kind of war than a war our nation was used to. You know firsthand the nature of the enemy. We face brutal men who celebrate murder, who incite suicide, and who would stop at nothing to destroy the liberties we cherish. You know that these enemies cannot be deterred by negotiations, or concessions, or appeals to reason. In this war, there's only one option—and that option is victory.

Since September the 11th, 2001, we have gone on the offensive against the terrorists. We have dealt the enemy a series of powerful blows. The terrorists are on the run, and we'll keep them on the run. Yet they're still active; they're still seeking to do us harm. The terrorists are patient and determined. And so are we. They're hoping we'll get complacent, and forget our responsibilities. Once again, they're proving that they do not understand our nation. The United States of America will never let down its guard.

George W. Bush, "President Discusses Patriot Act," speech given at Ohio State Highway Patrol Academy, June 9, 2005. www.whitehouse.gov.

This is a long war, and we have a comprehensive strategy to win it. We're taking the fight to the terrorists abroad, so we don't have to face them here at home. We're denying our enemies sanctuary, by making it clear that America will not tolerate regimes that harbor or support terrorists. We're stopping the terrorists from achieving the ideological victories they seek by spreading hope and freedom and reform across the broader Middle East. By advancing the cause of liberty, we'll lay the foundations for peace for generations to come.

To protect our country, we have to be right 100 percent of the time. To hurt us, the terrorists have to be right only once.

And one of the great honors as the President is to be the Commander-in-Chief of a fantastic United States military—made fantastic by the quality and the character of the men and women who wear the uniform. Thank you for serving.

As we wage the war on terror overseas, we'll remember where the war began—right here on American soil. In our free and open society, there is no such thing as perfect security. To protect our country, we have to be right 100 percent of the time. To hurt us, the terrorists have to be right only once. So we're working to answer that challenge every day, and we're making good progress toward securing the homeland.

Securing the Homeland

We've enhanced security at coastlines and borders and ports of entry. And we have more work to do. We've strengthened protections at our airports and chemical plants and highways and bridges and tunnels. And we got more work to do. We've made terrorism the top priority for law enforcement, and we've provided unprecedented resources to help folks like yourselves do their jobs.

Since 2001, we've more than tripled spending on home-land security, and we've increased funding more than tenfold for the first responders who protect our homeland. Law enforcement officers stand between our people and great dangers, and we're making sure you have the tools necessary to do your job.

The Patriot Act closed dangerous gaps in America's law enforcement and intelligence capabilities—gaps the terrorists exploited when they attacked us on September the 11th.

We've also improved our ability to track terrorists inside the United States. A vital part of that effort is called the USA Patriot Act. The Patriot Act closed dangerous gaps in America's law enforcement and intelligence capabilities—gaps the terrorists exploited when they attacked us on September 11th. Both houses of Congress passed the Patriot Act by overwhelming bipartisan majorities—98 out of 100 United States senators voted for the act. That's what we call bipartisanship. The Patriot Act was the clear, considered response of a nation at war, and I was proud to sign that piece of legislation.

Over the past three-and-a-half years, America's law enforcement and intelligence personnel have proved that the Patriot Act works, that it was an important piece of legislation. Since September the 11th, federal terrorism investigations have resulted in charges against more than 400 suspects, and more than half of those charged have been convicted. Federal, state, and local law enforcement have used the Patriot Act to break up terror cells in New York and Oregon and Virginia and in Florida. We've prosecuted terrorist operatives and supporters in California, in Texas, in New Jersey, in Illinois, and North Carolina and Ohio. These efforts have not always made the headlines, but they've made communities safer. The Patriot Act has accomplished exactly what it was designed to do—it has protected American liberty, and saved American lives.

Law enforcement officers should not be denied vital information their own colleagues already have.

The problem is, at the end of this year, 16 critical provisions of the Patriot Act are scheduled to expire. Some people call these "sunset provisions." That's a good name—because letting that—those provisions—expire would leave law enforcement in the dark. All 16 provisions are practical, important, and they are constitutional. Congress needs to renew them all—and this time, Congress needs to make the provisions permanent.

The Patriot Act Strengthens National Security

We need to renew the Patriot Act because it strengthens our national security in four important ways. First, we need to renew the critical provisions of the Patriot Act that authorize better sharing of information between law enforcement and intelligence. Before the Patriot Act, criminal investigators were separated from intelligence officers by a legal and bureaucratic wall. A federal prosecutor who investigated Osama bin Laden in the 1990s explained the challenge this way: "We could talk to citizens, local police officers, foreign police officers—we could even talk to al Qaeda members. But there was one group of people we were not permitted to talk to—the FBI agents across the street from us assigned to parallel intelligence investigations of Osama bin Laden and al Qaeda. That was a wall."

Finding our enemies in the war on terror is tough enough—law enforcement officers should not be denied vital information their own colleagues already have. The Patriot Act helped tear down this wall, and now law enforcement and intelligence officers are sharing information and working together, and bringing terrorists to justice.

Before the Patriot Act, it was easier to track the phone contacts of a drug dealer than the phone contacts of an enemy operative.

In many terrorism cases, information-sharing has made the difference between success and failure—and you have an example right here in Columbus, Ohio. Two years ago, a truck driver was charged with providing support to al Qaeda. His capture came after an investigation that relied on the Patriot Act, and on contributions from more than a dozen agencies in the Southern Ohio Joint Terrorism Task Force. And members of that task force are with us today. I want to thank you for your contribution to the safety of America, and you'll understand this story I'm about to tell.

For several years, Iman Faris posed as a law-abiding resident of Columbus. But in 2000, he traveled to Afghanistan and met Osama bin Laden at an al Qaeda training camp. Faris helped the terrorists research airplanes and handle cash and purchase supplies. In 2002, he met Khalid Shaykh Muhammad—the mastermind of the September 11th attacks—and he agreed to take part in an al Qaeda plot to destroy a New York City bridge.

After Faris returned to the United States, federal investigators used the Patriot Act to follow his trail. They used new information-sharing provisions to piece together details about his time in Afghanistan, and his plan to launch an attack on the United States. They used the Patriot Act to discover that Faris had cased possible targets in New York and that he'd reported his findings to al Qaeda. In the spring of 2003, the FBI confronted Faris, and presented the case they had built against him. The case against him was so strong that Faris chose to cooperate, and he spent the next several weeks telling authorities about his al Qaeda association. Faris pled guilty to the charges against him. And today, instead of planning terror attacks against the American people, Iman Faris is sitting in an American prison.

If we have good tools to fight street crime and fraud, law enforcement should have the same tools to fight terrorism.

The agents and prosecutors who used the Patriot Act to put Faris behind bars did superb work, and they know what a difference information-sharing made. Here is what one FBI agent said—he said, "The Faris case would not have happened without sharing information." That information-sharing was made possible by the Patriot Act. Another investigator on the case said, "We never would have had the lead to begin with." You have proved that good teamwork is critical in protecting America. For the sake of our national security, Congress must not rebuild a wall between law enforcement and intelligence.

Allowing Use of Same Tools Against Terrorists as Against Criminals

Second, we need to renew the critical provisions of the Patriot Act that allow investigators to use the same tools against terrorists that they already use against other criminals. Before the Patriot Act, it was easier to track the phone contacts of a drug dealer than the phone contacts of an enemy operative. Before the Patriot Act, it was easier to get the credit card receipts of a tax cheat than an al Qaeda bankroller. Before the Patriot Act, agents could use wiretaps to investigate a person committing mail fraud, but not to investigate a foreign terrorist. The Patriot Act corrected all these pointless double standards—and America is safer as a result.

One tool that has been especially important to law enforcement is called a roving wiretap. Roving wiretaps allow investigators to follow suspects who frequently change their means of communications. These wiretaps must be approved by a judge, and they have been used for years to catch drug dealers and other criminals. Yet, before the Patriot Act, agents investigating terrorists had to get a separate authorization for each phone they wanted to tap. That means terrorists could elude law enforcement by simply purchasing a new cell phone. The Patriot Act fixed the problem by allowing terrorism investigators to use the same wiretaps that were already being [used] against drug kingpins and mob bosses. The theory here is straightforward: If we have good tools to fight street crime and fraud, law enforcement should have the same tools to fight terrorism.

Third, we need to renew the critical provisions of the Patriot Act that updated the law to meet high-tech threats like computer espionage and cyberterrorism. Before the Patriot Act, Internet providers who notified federal authorities about threatening e-mails ran the risk of getting sued. The Patriot Act modernized the law to protect Internet companies who voluntarily disclose information to save lives.

It's common sense reform, and it's delivered results. In April 2004, a man sent an e-mail to an Islamic center in El Paso, and threatened to burn the mosque to the ground in three days. Before the Patriot Act, the FBI could have spent a week or more waiting for the information they needed. Thanks to the Patriot Act, an Internet provider was able to provide the information quickly and without fear of a lawsuit—and the FBI arrested the man before he could fulfill his—fulfill his threat.

Terrorists are using every advantage they can to inflict harm. Terrorists are using every advantage of 21st century technology, and Congress needs to ensure that our law enforcement can use that same advantage, as well.

The Patriot Act Protects Civil Liberties

Finally, we need to renew the critical provisions of the Patriot Act that protect our civil liberties. The Patriot Act was written with clear safeguards to ensure the law is applied fairly. The judicial branch has a strong oversight role. Law enforcement officers need a federal judge's permission to wiretap a foreign terrorist's phone, a federal judge's permission to track his calls, or a federal judge's permission to search his property. Officers must meet strict standards to use any of these tools. And these standards are fully consistent with the Constitution of the U.S.

Congress also oversees the application of the Patriot Act. Congress has recently created a federal board to ensure that the Patriot Act and other laws respect privacy and civil liberties. And I'll soon name five talented Americans to serve on that board. Attorney General Gonzales delivers regular reports on the Patriot Act to the House and the Senate, and the Department of Justice has answered hundreds of questions from members of Congress. One Senator, Dianne Feinstein of California, has worked with civil rights groups to monitor my administration's use of the Patriot Act. Here's what she said: "We've scrubbed the area, and I have no reported abuses." Remember that the next time you hear someone make an unfair criticism of this important, good law. The Patriot Act has not diminished American liberties; the Patriot Act has helped to defend American liberties.

Every day the men and women of law enforcement use the Patriot Act to keep America safe. It's the nature of your job that many of your most important achievements must remain secret. Americans will always be grateful for the risks you take, and for the determination you bring to this high calling. You have done your job. Now those of us in Washington have to do our job. The House and Senate are moving forward with the process to renew the Patriot Act. My message to Congress is clear: The terrorist threats against us will not expire at the end of the year, and neither should the protections of the Patriot Act.

I want to thank you for letting me come and talk about this important piece of legislation. I want to thank you for being on the front lines of securing this country. May God bless you and your families. And may God continue to bless our nation. Thank you very much.

The Patriot Act Gives Investigators Tools for Fighting in the 21st Century

Alberto Gonzales

Alberto Gonzales was the attorney general of the United States from February 2005 until September 17, 2007, when he resigned under criticism, facing allegations of perjury before Congress. Gonzales was the first Hispanic to hold the position. He previously served on the Texas Supreme Court.

For more than two centuries, our Nation's love for freedom has defined the course of American history. During that time, we may not have always lived up to our best ideals, but our love for liberty and individual rights has always lit our way toward a better, more inclusive Nation.

Half a world away, the people of Iraq and Afghanistan are experiencing today [in 2005], for the first time, the power and potential of freedom. Even in the face of threats of violence, they are taking steps toward free speech, free assembly, and civil liberty.

Only a few weeks ago the world watched in awe and admiration as Iraqi voters held aloft their blue-tipped fingers to celebrate their first free elections. We will not forget the bravery of women—mothers, daughters, and sisters—who risked death to walk to their polling places. And I suspect many of us will look back with emotion at the tears of joy shed by expatriate Iraqi voters who never thought they would live to see a free, democratic Iraq come into being.

Courageous Iraqis have reminded every American that democracy is built on the exchange of ideas through debate, dis-

Alberto Gonzales, "Prepared Remarks of Attorney General Alberto Gonzales Address to National Association of Counties Legislative Conference Washington, D.C. March 7, 2005," Department of Justice, March 7, 2005. www.usdoj.gov.

cussion, and dialogue. Even when there is disagreement, respect and tolerance for differing views can transform the heart and heal the land.

I think we can all recognize that the work of prevention is far better than the pain and devastation that would flow from another terrorist attack.

Most of all, they have reminded us all what a privilege it is to be part of the great debate that is democracy.

In a few weeks, we will begin here a serious discussion with implications for our Nation's future, as Congress faces the opportunity to reauthorize the USA PATRIOT Act.

In this dialogue, our goal remains what it was three-and-a-half years ago when the Administration and Congress worked together to pass this law: to give law enforcement the tools they need to keep America safe, while honoring our values and our Constitution.

This debate has considerable importance for county officials across our Nation. Whether we, as public servants, serve in Federal, state, or county government, our most fundamental obligation is to protect the people we serve. Simply put, without security, government cannot deliver, nor can the people enjoy, the prosperity and opportunities that flow from freedom and democracy.

Some local officials have focused only on the investigative tools of the Act without considering the built-in safeguards that protect our liberties.

As county officials, I know you are dedicated to the safety and security of all your constituents. Since September 11, [2001,] you have responded to the need to increase homeland security and to support law enforcement and first responders. And I thank you.

While these years of continuing preparation have been expensive and challenging, I think we can all recognize that the work of prevention is far better than the pain and devastation that would flow from another terrorist attack.

The PATRIOT Act Has Proven Vital to Defense

As you consider further your county's own role in protecting our Nation, it is important to remember that the PATRIOT Act has already proven a vital part of our defense of protecting lives and liberties.

Unfortunately, certain provisions of this law have attracted some adverse attention. Some local officials have focused only on the investigative tools of the Act without considering the built-in safeguards that protect our liberties. I suspect this has motivated some counties and cities to pass resolutions against the PATRIOT Act.

For the past three years, U.S. attorneys have been available to speak before county and city council meetings about the constitutional protections in and the importance of the PATRIOT Act. I have been told that, in a few cities, U.S. attorneys' efforts to be heard have been refused.

As the months and years since September 11 pass, complacency becomes our enemy.

If true, I am concerned that some local officials have cast votes relating to the PATRIOT Act based on misinformation or a lack of information.

I know that you are conscientious about serving your communities and your constituents, and that whenever you are faced with important issues you want to have the best information available to you.

Today [March 7, 2005] I am going to give you facts I hope will inform your decisions regarding the PATRIOT Act.

Let me begin by asking you to remember the liberties we seek to protect, the lives we are sworn to defend, and the brutal lessons taught by September 11.

Over the last three years, we have made great progress in the war against terror. Thanks to the hard work of millions of men and women in Federal, state, and local law enforcement, in our intelligence community, and in the military, we are safer and more secure.

But our successes confront us with a new challenge: As the months and years since September 11 pass, complacency becomes our enemy. We face the temptation to think that the terrorist threat is receding and that September 11 was just one tragic day—a once-in-a-lifetime event not likely to be repeated.

Based on the intelligence we have collected, we know that our enemies do not view September 11 that way. They remember, and they want to do worse.

The PATRIOT Act has addressed critical vulnerabilities in America's pre-September 11th defenses.

We, too, must remember the horror, the outrage, the sadness of that day—and use these emotions to motivate us to stop our enemies from duplicating their attacks. . . .

As we begin our discussion about the PATRIOT Act, we must also understand how our enemies saw September 11th, and how they view this conflict.

As one radical supporter of Al Qaeda stated in a fatwa [an Islamic scholar's ruling or law] after September 11: "It is astonishing to mourn the [American] victims as being innocents. Those victims may be classified as infidel Americans, which do not deserve being mourned, because each American, as to his relation to American government, is a warrior, or supporter, in money or opinion. It is legitimate to kill all of them."

These "legitimate" targets referred to are our moms and dads, sons and daughters, neighbors and loved ones.

We know . . . that terrorist networks use computers, email, and cellular phones to cloak their operations, here and abroad.

Defending American Freedoms

Our enemy has no respect for life, for civil or religious liberty. They do not believe in the right to conscience, or personal choice.

These are values we prize—simple freedoms your constituents and our fellow citizens hold precious: From standing up to speak out at a school board meeting to writing your local council members for help, from visiting a child's teacher to writing your congressional representative.

My job as Attorney General is to defend every day those values and the freedoms enshrined in our Bill of Rights and our Constitution.

My workdays begin with a morning intelligence briefing. With FBI Director Mueller, we review the latest counterterrorism intelligence and situation analyses and report to the President our Nation's progress in the fight against terrorism.

Unfortunately, a small but vocal minority has attempted to mischaracterize the PATRIOT Act.

In my capacity as White House Counsel and now as Attorney General, I have met and heard from many of the men and women winning the war on terror for our Nation. They tell me that the PATRIOT Act is very important in our law enforcement and intelligence efforts. They tell me that without this law, many of our most important successes would not have been possible. The PATRIOT Act has addressed critical vulnerabilities in America's pre-September 11th defenses.

First, it lowered the artificial and unwise bureaucratic wall that had prevented law enforcement and the intelligence community from sharing information about terrorist movements and plots.

Second, it modernized and gave investigators legal tools for fighting in the 21st century. These are tools, such as "multipoint wiretaps," which have proven themselves time and again in the fight against drug smugglers, mobsters, and other criminals. They have long been sanctioned by our courts, but were not available for national security investigations until the PATRIOT Act.

We know, for instance, that terrorist networks use computers, email, and cellular phones to cloak their operations, here and abroad. They are trained to switch phones and email accounts in order to make it harder for us to track them.

For more than three years, there has not been one verified civil rights abuse under the PATRIOT Act.

Under the PATRIOT Act, officials may now obtain court approval to use a "multipoint wiretap" to track a terror suspect's phone communications, even when the suspected terrorist switches, changes, or abandons phones to avoid detection. These and other common-sense measures included in the PATRIOT Act have helped our Federal, state, and county officials make America safer.

Unfortunately, a small but vocal minority has attempted to mischaracterize the PATRIOT Act. The critics have dealt in conjecture and hypotheticals. We can point to solid results, saved lives, and a Nation that is safer. For more than three years, there has not been one verified civil rights abuse under the PATRIOT Act.

As Senator Dianne Feinstein has stated, quote, "I have never had a single abuse of the Patriot Act reported to me. My staff e-mailed the ACLU and asked them for instances of actual abuses. They e-mailed back and said they had none."

I want to encourage you to come forward if you or your constituents have ever experienced an abuse under the PATRIOT Act. If there are violations, I want to know about them.

But the Act has helped us considerably in the war on terror. Thanks to this law, America's law enforcement and the intelligence communities were able to work together to break up the "Portland Seven" terrorist cell. Members of this terrorist cell had attempted to travel to Afghanistan in 2001 and 2002 to fight with the Taliban and Al Qaeda against the United States. Because law enforcement was allowed to conduct surveillance on one member of the cell, agents and officers knew they could prevent an attack as well as continue to gather evidence against other operatives in the terror cell.

The PATRIOT Act Helps Solve Crimes

Some commentators have claimed that the PATRIOT Act violates personal Internet privacy. But the law allows Internet Service Providers to aid law enforcement voluntarily, and only in emergency situations. Such voluntary cooperation allows for businesses to protect consumer information as well as allow for swift action when lives are on the line.

Here is one example of how this can help us solve crimes. Only a few months ago, the Nation was shocked by the tragedy of Bobbie Jo Stinnett. Bobbie Jo had been eight months pregnant when she was found strangled to death in her Missouri home. Her unborn daughter had been cut out of her womb with a kitchen knife.

Police officers examined a computer found in Bobbie Jo's home. They discovered that she had been active on the Internet in connection with her dog-breeding business. As the investigation intensified, the officers found an exchange from a message board between Bobbie Jo and someone who called herself Darlene Fischer. Fischer claimed to be interested in a dog. She had asked Bobbie Jo for directions to her house for a meeting on December 16—the same day as the murder.

Using a PATRIOT Act provision, FBI agents and examiners at the Regional Computer Forensic Laboratory in Kansas City were able to trace Darlene Fischer's messages to a server in Topeka, find Darlene Fischer's email address, and then trace it to a house in Melvern, Kansas. Darlene Fischer's real name was in fact Lisa Montgomery. Montgomery was arrested and subsequently confessed.

Thanks in part to the hard work of law enforcement and the technological advances of the PATRIOT Act, baby Victoria Jo Stinnett was found alive—less than 24 hours after she was cut from her mother's womb.

In this criminal case, the PATRIOT Act helped save one baby's life. In the case of terrorism worldwide, such voluntary cooperation and speed can save thousands of lives. If these tools can be used to stop child molesters and kidnappers as well as terrorist financiers and Al Qaeda operatives, we will all be able to live in an America that is safer, more secure, and more free.

Some critics have claimed that the PATRIOT Act endangers our civil liberties. Let me be clear that I think we should be free—and we are free—to question the exercise of government power when we believe it may infringe on our privacy or our civil liberties. Such debate is good and healthy for our democracy. But debate should be based on facts. And in 2004, the Patriot Act was used to protect the lives and liberties of members of the El Paso Islamic Center. Thirty-year-old Jared Bjarnason sent an email message threatening to burn the mosque to the ground if hostages in Iraq were not freed within three days.

Acting quickly, FBI agents used a provision of the PATRIOT Act to identify Bjarnason as the source of the threat. Without this tool, law enforcement would have had to obtain a separate search warrant from each service provider through which the email traveled. In the case of Bjarnason, such a string of search warrants could have taken 30 days—far beyond his threatened deadline. Bjarnason was found, arrested, and has pleaded guilty.

The PATRIOT Act Protects Civil Liberties

As these examples show, the PATRIOT Act protects civil liberties as well as American lives. What is often left out of the critics' accusations are the many safeguards built into the law itself.

The PATRIOT Act requires judicial approval for delayed-notification search warrants. Courts can only allow these search warrants in the face of threats such as the death or physical harm to an individual, evidence tampering, witness intimidation, flight from prosecution, or serious jeopardy to an investigation. At all times, the Government is subject to the jurisdiction and supervision of a federal judge.

The PATRIOT Act requires investigators to apply and receive federal court permission to obtain a pen register or trap-and-trace device—which simply provide investigators with routing information, such as incoming and outgoing phone numbers from a phone. There is no collection of the content of the communication under the Act.

The PATRIOT Act requires investigators to obtain a court order to examine business records in the course of a national security investigation or to protect against international terrorism. Such court orders may not be obtained to investigate ordinary crimes, or even for domestic terrorism.

The PATRIOT Act allows individuals recourse if they believe their rights are abused. In addition, the Justice Department's Inspector General is required by law to designate one official to review information and complaints alleging the abuse or violation of civil liberties by Justice officials.

Finally, the PATRIOT Act requires me, every six months, to report to the House Judiciary Committee and Senate Judiciary Committee the number of applications made for orders requiring the production of business records under the PATRIOT Act.

As these examples illustrate, the PATRIOT Act not only fully respects the rights and liberties of America, but the law contains built-in safeguards that ensure the protection of our rights.

As Attorney General, it is my job to fight for a stronger, safer Nation guided by the rule of law, a dedication to justice, and opportunity for all. Each day, the men and women of the Justice Department defend the civil liberties that make America so special. And we work to ensure that terrorists do not endanger the peace and freedom so important to the exercise of our precious rights.

As the cause of freedom expands around the globe, it is my honor to work to see that it expands here at home. I believe that our war on terrorism and the PATRIOT Act are critical to this cause. As we move forward in discussing its reauthorization, I welcome the debate and look forward to hearing the views of others. The President has said we must reauthorize the PATRIOT Act. If some have suggestions for improvements to our laws that make America safer, I would be interested in hearing those. But mindful of the tragedy of September 11, I will not support changes in the law that would make America more vulnerable to terrorist attacks.

Thank you again for having me here today.

May God bless you and your families, may He continue to guide our democratic debate and dialogue, and may He continue to bless the United States of America.

The Patriot Act Extends Existing Wiretap Powers to Investigation of Terrorism

Michael Sullivan

As of 2008, Michael Sullivan was the U.S. attorney for the District of Massachusetts, in which role he represented the United States in civil and criminal litigation in the District Court that has jurisdiction over Massachusetts.

If sections 201 and 202 [of the Patriot Act] are allowed to sunset, we will lose valuable tools that allow law enforcement to investigate a full range of terrorism-related crimes. Paradoxically, these tools would be unavailable in criminal terrorism investigations of offenses involving chemical weapons, cyberterrorism, or weapons of mass destruction, but would be available to investigate traditional crimes such as drug offenses, mail fraud, and passport fraud. This would be a senseless approach. Because it is absolutely vital that the Justice Department have all appropriate tools at its disposal to investigate terrorism crimes, I am here today to ask you to make permanent sections 201 and 202 of the USA PATRIOT Act. In addition, if section 223 were allowed to expire, then individuals whose privacy might have been violated through the use of these tools would be denied an important avenue for redress.

The Wiretap Statute

In the criminal law enforcement context, federal investigators have long been able to obtain court orders to intercept wire communications (voice communications over a phone) and oral communications (voice communications in person) to investigate numerous criminal offenses listed in the federal

Michael Sullivan, statement before the Subcommittee on Crime, Terrorism and Homeland Security, Committee on the Judiciary, U.S. House of Representatives, May 3, 2005.

wiretap statute. The listed offenses include traditional crimes, including drug crimes, mail fraud, and passport fraud. Prior to the enactment of the USA PATRIOT Act, however, certain extremely serious crimes that terrorists are likely to commit, such as those involving chemical weapons, the killing of United States nationals abroad, the use of weapons of mass destruction, and the provision of material support to foreign terrorist organizations, were not among them. This prevented law enforcement authorities from using many forms of electronic surveillance to investigate these serious criminal offenses. As a result, law enforcement could obtain, under appropriate circumstances, a court order to intercept phone communications in a passport fraud investigation, but not a criminal investigation of terrorists using chemical weapons or murdering a United States national abroad.

Section 201 of the USA PATRIOT Act ended this anomaly in the law by amending the criminal wiretap statute. It added the following terrorism-related crimes to the list of wiretap predicates: 1) chemical weapons offenses; 2) murders and other acts of violence against United States national occurring outside the United States; 3) the use of weapons of mass destruction; 4) violent acts of terrorism transcending national borders; 5) financial transactions with countries that support terrorism; and 6) material support of terrorists and terrorist organizations. There were also two other offenses that were subsequently added to this list which included bombings of places of public use, government facilities, public transportation systems, and infrastructure facilities, and financing of terrorism.

Section 201 of the USA PATRIOT Act preserved all of the pre-existing standards in the wiretap statute. For example, law enforcement still must apply for and receive a court order; establish probable cause to believe an individual is committing, has committed, or is about to commit a particular predicate offense; establish probable cause to believe that particular communications concerning that offense will be obtained through the wiretap; and establish that "normal investigative procedures" have been tried and failed or reasonably appear to be unlikely to succeed or are too dangerous.

If wiretaps are an appropriate investigative tool to be utilized in cases involving bribery, gambling, and obscenity, then surely investigators should be able to use them when investigating the use of weapons of mass destruction.

Since the enactment of the USA PATRIOT Act, Justice Department investigators have utilized Section 201 to investigate, among other things, potential weapons of mass destruction offenses as well as the provision of material support to terrorists. In total, as of March 10, 2005, the Department utilized section 201 on four occasions. These four uses occurred in two separate investigations. One of those cases involved an Imperial Wizard of the White Knights of the Ku Klux Klan who attempted to purchase hand grenades for the purpose of bombing abortion clinics and was subsequently convicted of numerous explosives and firearms charges.

Section 201 is extremely valuable to the Justice Department's counterterrorism efforts because it enables criminal investigators to gather information using this crucial technique, subject to all of the requirements of the wiretap statute, when investigating terrorism-related crimes, and ensuring that these offenses are thoroughly investigated and effectively prosecuted. If wiretaps are an appropriate investigative tool to be utilized in cases involving bribery, gambling, and obscenity, then surely investigators should be able to use them when investigating the use of weapons of mass destruction, chemical weapons offenses, and other terrorism-related offenses.

Computer Crimes

Just as many traditional terrorism-related offenses were not listed as wiretap predicates before the passage of the USA PATRIOT Act, neither were many important cybercrime or cyberterrorism offenses, offenses concerning which law enforcement must remain vigilant and prepared in the 21st century. Therefore, once again, while criminal investigators could obtain wiretap orders to monitor wire and oral communications to investigate gambling offenses or other crimes, but they could not use such techniques in appropriate cases involving certain serious computer crimes. Section 202 of the USA PATRIOT Act eliminated this anomaly by allowing law enforcement to use pre-existing wiretap authorities to investigate felony offenses under the Computer Fraud and Abuse Act, and brought the criminal code up to date with modern technology.

As with section 201, section 202 of the USA PATRIOT Act preserved all of the preexisting standards in the wiretap statute, ensuring that law enforcement still must apply and receive a court order; establish probable cause to believe an individual is committing or about to commit the predicate offense; establish probable cause to believe that particular communications about the offense will be obtained through the wiretap; and establish that normal investigative procedures have been tried and failed or reasonably appear to be unlikely to succeed or are too dangerous.

As of March 10, 2005, the Justice Department had used section 202 of the USA PATRIOT Act on two occasions. These two uses occurred in a computer fraud investigation that eventually broadened to include drug trafficking. If section 202 were allowed to expire, then investigators would not be able to obtain wiretap orders to investigate many important cybercrime and cyberterrorism offenses, resulting in a criminal code that is dangerously out of date compared to modern technology.

Protection Against Abuse

Prior to the enactment of the USA PATRIOT Act, individuals were permitted only in limited circumstances to file a cause of action and collect money damages against the United States if government officials unlawfully disclosed sensitive information collected through the use of court-approved investigative tools. For example, while those engaging in illegal wiretapping or electronic surveillance were subject to civil liability, those improperly disclosing information obtained from lawful pen register orders or warrants for stored electronic mail generally could not be sued. Section 223 of the USA PATRIOT Act remedied this inequitable situation by creating an important mechanism for deterring the improper disclosure of sensitive information and providing redress for individuals whose privacy might be violated by such disclosures.

Under section 223, a person harmed by a willful violation of the criminal wiretap statute or improper use and disclosure of information contained in the Foreign Intelligence Surveillance Act [FISA] may file a claim against the United States for at least $10,000 in damages, plus costs. The section also broadened the circumstances under which administrative discipline may be imposed upon a federal official who improperly handled sensitive information by requiring the agency to initiate a proceeding in order to determine the appropriate disciplinary action.

I know firsthand how valuable wiretaps are to the investigation and prosecution of serious criminal offenses. There is no logical reason why these valuable tools should not be extended to allow law enforcement to protect our citizens from terrorism-related offenses as well.

To date, no complaints have been filed against Department employees pursuant to section 223. This is a reflection of the professionalism of the Department's employees as well as their commitment to the rule of law. Although there have been no allegations of abuse[s] under this section, it is important that section 223 remain in effect as it provides an important disincentive to those who would unlawfully disclose intercepted communications. Most everyone who has reviewed this provision agrees that it is a valuable tool that should certainly be renewed. In addition, section 223 clearly demonstrates the PATRIOT Act's concern, not just the security of the United States, but also for the civil liberties of its citizens.

Thank you once again for the opportunity to discuss sections 201, 202, and 223 of the USA PATRIOT Act. These provisions are critical to the Department's efforts to protect Americans from terrorism. From my experience as a prosecutor, I know firsthand how valuable wiretaps are to the investigation and prosecution of serious criminal offenses. There is no logical reason why these valuable tools should not be extended to allow law enforcement to protect our citizens from terrorism-related offenses as well.

Tracking Phone Calls Allows Investigators to Link Conspirators

Mary Beth Buchanan

Mary Beth Buchanan was, as of 2008, the U.S. attorney for the Western District of Pennsylvania. In that role, she oversaw the prosecution of all federal crimes, and the litigation of civil matters in which the federal government had an interest, throughout that district.

Mr. Chairman, Ranking Member Scott, Members of the Subcommittee, thank you for asking me here today. I am Mary Beth Buchanan, the United States Attorney in the Western District of Pennsylvania and the Director of the Executive Office for United States Attorneys. It is an honor to appear before you today to discuss how the Department has used the important provisions of the USA PATRIOT Act to better combat terrorism and other serious criminal conduct. I will specifically focus today on two of the provisions that are the subject of today's hearing—Section 214 and Section 225 of the USA PATRIOT Act—since those are two provisions that harmonized tools used in terrorism investigations with tools that have been used routinely and effectively in criminal prosecutions long before the passage of the USA PATRIOT Act.

Pen Register and Trap-and-Trace Devices

Section 214 of the USA PATRIOT Act allows the government to obtain a pen register order in national security investigations where the information likely is relevant to an international terrorism or espionage investigation. This provision is similar to the 1986 criminal pen register statute that has been

Mary Beth Buchanan, statement before the Subcommittee on Crime, Terrorism and Homeland Security, Committee on the Judiciary, U.S. House of Representatives, April 26, 2005.

frequently used by criminal prosecutors to obtain pen registers and trap-and-trace devices in a variety of criminal investigations. A pen register is a device that can track dialing, routing, addressing, and signaling information about a communication—for example, which numbers are dialed from a particular telephone. Pen registers are not used to collect the content of communications. Similarly, a trap-and-trace device tracks numbers used to call a particular telephone, without monitoring the substance or content of the telephone conversation. Both devices are routinely used in criminal investigations where, in order to obtain the necessary order authorizing use of the device, the government must show simply that the information sought is relevant to an ongoing investigation.

Pen registers and trap-and-trace devices have long been used as standard preliminary investigative tools in a variety of criminal investigations and prosecutions. In many instances, these tools are used as one of the first steps in a criminal investigation with the information gathered used to determine if more intrusive forms of surveillance, such as search warrants or wiretaps, are justified. Use of these tools may often times lead investigators and prosecutors to additional suspects or targets in an investigation because of their important ability to allow prosecutors to link defendants or "connect the dots" in a conspiracy or other type of criminal offense.

To obtain a pen register or trap-and-trace device ..., a criminal prosecutor must certify that the information sought is relevant to an ongoing criminal investigation, and upon that certification, the court enters an *ex parte* order [an order not disclosed to the other party] authorizing the installation and use of a pen register or a trap-and-trace device. There is no requirement that the court make a probable cause finding. Under long-settled Supreme Court precedent, the use of pen registers does not constitute a "search" within the meaning of the Fourth Amendment. As such, the Constitution does not require that the government obtain court approval before installing a pen register. The absence of a probable cause requirement is justified because the devices merely obtain information that is voluntarily disclosed to the telephone service provider. Therefore, there is no reasonable expectation of privacy in the information.

Patriot Act Made Investigation of Terrorism Easier

Currently [as of 2005] under FISA, government officials similarly may seek a court order for a pen register or trap-and-trace device to gather foreign intelligence information or information about international terrorism or espionage. Prior to enactment of the USA PATRIOT Act, however, FISA required government personnel to certify not just that the information they sought was relevant to an intelligence investigation, but also that the facilities to be monitored had been used or were about to be used to contact a foreign agent or an agent of a foreign power, such as a terrorist or spy. Thus, it was much more difficult to obtain an effective pen register or trap-and-trace order in an international terrorism investigation than in a criminal investigation.

There is no good reason for investigators to have fewer tools to use in terrorism investigations than they have long used in criminal investigations.

Section 214 of the USA PATRIOT Act brought authorities for terrorism and other foreign intelligence investigations more into line with similar criminal authorities by permitting court approval of FISA pen registers and trap-and-trace orders even though an applicant might be unable to certify at that stage of an investigation that the facilities themselves, such as phones, are used by foreign agents or those engaged in international terrorist or clandestine intelligence activities. Significantly, however, applicants must still certify that the devices are likely to obtain foreign intelligence information not concerning a U.S. person, or information relevant to an international terrorism investigation. Section 214 streamlined the process for obtaining pen registers under FISA while preserving the existing court-order requirement that is evaluated by the same relevance standard as in the criminal context. Now as before, investigators cannot install a pen register unless they apply for and receive permission from the FISA Court. In addition, Section 214 explicitly safeguards First Amendment rights. It requires that any investigation of a United States person not be conducted solely upon the basis of activities protected by the First Amendment to the Constitution. As a result, the Department of Justice must satisfy the FISA Court that its investigation is not solely based upon First Amendment protected activity, which requires the Department to inform the Court of the justification for the investigation.

If Section 214 were allowed to expire, it would be more difficult to obtain a pen register order in an international terrorism investigation than in a criminal investigation, and investigators would have a harder time developing leads in important terrorism investigations.

Patriot Act Provides Immunity from Liability to Those Who Assist in Terrorist Investigations

Section 225 of the USA PATRIOT Act also harmonized the FISA context and criminal prosecutions—in this case extending an important provision used for years in criminal prosecutions to the FISA context. The United States may obtain electronic surveillance and physical search orders from the FISA Court concerning an entity or individual whom the court finds probable cause to believe is an agent of a foreign power. Generally, however, as in the case of criminal wiretaps and electronic surveillance, the United States requires the assistance of private communications providers to carry out such court orders. In the criminal and civil contexts, those who disclose information pursuant to a subpoena or court order are generally exempted from liability. For example, those assisting the government in carrying out criminal investigative wiretaps are provided with immunity from civil liability. This immunity is important because it helps to secure the prompt cooperation of private parties with law enforcement officers to ensure the effective implementation of court orders.

Prior to the passage of the USA PATRIOT Act, however, while those assisting in the implementation of criminal wiretaps were provided with immunity, no similar immunity protected those companies and individuals assisting the government in carrying out surveillance orders issued by the FISA Court under FISA. Section 225 ended this anomaly by providing immunity to those who assist the government in implementing FISA surveillance orders, thus ensuring that such entities and individuals will comply with orders issued by the FISA Court without delay. This immunity is important because it helps to secure the prompt cooperation of private parties, such as telephone companies, whose assistance is necessary for the effective implementation of court orders. For example, in the investigation of an espionage subject, the FBI was able to convince a company to assist in the installation of technical equipment pursuant to a FISA order by providing a letter outlining the immunity from civil liability associated with complying with the FISA order. Section 225 has been praised for protecting those companies and individuals who are simply fulfilling their legal obligations. If section 225 is allowed to expire, it would be more difficult for the Department of Justice to implement FISA surveillance orders in a timely and effective manner. Because Section 225 simply extends to the FISA context the exemption long applied in the civil and criminal contexts, where individuals who disclose information pursuant to a subpoena or court order generally are immune from liability for disclosure, it should be made permanent.

I thank you for inviting me here and giving me the opportunity to explain in concrete terms how the USA PATRIOT Act has changed the way we fight terrorism. I hope you agree that there is no good reason for investigators to have fewer tools to use in terrorism investigations than they have long used in criminal investigations. Fortunately, the USA PATRIOT Act was passed by Congress to correct these flaws in the system. Now that we have fixed this process, we can't go back. We must continue to pursue the terrorists with every legal means available. The law enforcement community needs the important tools of the USA PATRIOT Act to continue to keep our nation safe from attack.

The Patriot Act Was Crucial in Preventing a Potential Attack

Terence P. Jeffrey

Terence P. Jeffrey is editor at large for Human Events *magazine.*

Homegrown terrorist Jeffrey Leon Battle considered America the "land of the kaffirs," or unbelievers, and the American people "pigs." He once lamented to an acquaintance—who happened to be a government informant—that the Sept. 11, 2001, terrorist attacks did not sufficiently damage the U.S. economy. "This is the land of the enemy," he said of his own country in a May 8, 2002, conversation secretly recorded by the government. He explained to a friend how his "burning desire" to become an Islamic martyr had inspired his aborted quest to join forces with al Qaeda in Afghanistan, where he could kill American troops.

Battle, now 35, is serving an 18-year prison sentence for conspiring to wage war against the United States, a crime to which he confessed and pleaded guilty. But members of Congress who are stalling on renewing the Patriot Act and attacking President Bush for ordering the National Security Agency to intercept al Qaeda-linked communications in and out of the United States could learn something from studying the activities and communications of the Portland Seven terrorist cell that Battle and others began forming in Oregon in the months before—that's right, before—the Sept. 11, 2001, terrorist attacks. . . .

In his May 8, 2002, conversation with a government informant, federal prosecutors said in a sentencing memorandum, Battle discussed this plan. "If every time [the Israelis] hurt or harm a Muslim over there [in Palestine] you go into that

Terence P. Jeffrey, "Terrorist Blamed His Failure on Bush," *Human Events*, February 13, 2006. Reproduced by permission.

synagogue and hurt one over here, okay, they're gonna say, wait a minute, we gotta stop, we're seeing a connection here, okay . . . ," said Battle. "We were going to hit all at the same time as each other. . . . We were willing to get caught or die if we could do [murder] at least 100 or 1,000, big numbers."

All along the way, these terrorists left an electronic trail.

The day after this conversation, prosecutors say in their memo, "Battle spoke of his preference to commit an act of mass murder by staging a raid, as opposed to a suicide mission, because he wanted to be alive to see the damage inflicted."

Squad of Death

After the 9/11 attacks, however, Battle and five other members of the Portland cell decided that rather than attack inside the U.S. they would travel via China and Pakistan to Afghanistan to join forces with al Qaeda there. In the late fall of 2001, calling themselves by the Arabic name Katibat Al-Mawt ("The Squad of Death"), the group made their way from Portland, Ore., toward the China-Pakistan frontier. When they failed after repeated attempts to gain entry into Pakistan from China, two of the six immediately returned to the United States. Three remained for a while in various parts of Asia, where Battle, at least, continued his futile efforts to gain entry into Pakistan. One of the six eventually did make it to Pakistan.

All along the way, these terrorists left an electronic trail.

Battle's former wife, October Martinique Lewis, the seventh member of the gang, had stayed behind in Portland. She repeatedly wired Battle money in Hong Kong, Beijing, and, finally, Bangladesh, often informing Battle via e-mail after sending the wire. When she later pleaded guilty to money laundering, the Justice Department said in a statement that "she knew the money she wired was going to be used to support continuing attempts to enter Afghanistan to fight in jihad for the Taliban against the United States."

Battle . . . was obviously worried that his telephone calls back to the United States might be intercepted.

When then-30-year-old Patrice Lumumba Ford, who, like Battle, would later plead guilty to conspiring to wage war against the United States, gave up trying to cross from China into Pakistan, he returned to Oregon. There he became a con duit for money for Habis Al Saoub, whom The Squad of Death called their "emir," or leader. . . .

When Squad of Death member Ford arrived back in Portland from China in late 2001, he twice wired money to Al Saoub. On Nov. 20, 2001, he sent him $500, and on Jan. 3, 2002, he sent him $483. In both instances, Al Saoub was still in China.

Affluent American Terrorist

Squad of Death member Maher "Mike" Hawash, a 37-year-old naturalized American software engineer born in the West Bank city of Nablus, had done very well in the United States. . . . But as with Osama bin Laden himself, affluence did not turn Hawash away from terrorism, and he eventually pleaded guilty to conspiracy to supply services to the Taliban.

He, too, had an electronic international communication with Al Saoub. "After Hawash returned to the United States, he received a phone call from Al Saoub asking for money," prosecutors alleged in their sentencing memo for the Battle and Ford cases. "Hawash arranged for $2,000 to be sent by someone in Nablus in the West Bank area of Palestine to defendant Al Saoub in China."

And Hawash was not the only person in the United States that Squad of Death "Emir" Al Saoub telephoned from overseas while on his trek to Afghanistan. On Jan. 4, 2002, according to McCartney's affidavit, "Sofiane Benziadi was arrested for immigration violations." When interviewed four days later by federal investigators, "Benziadi stated that he had heard about several American males leaving the United States to travel to Afghanistan and fight beside the Taliban. . . . Benziadi went on to explain that he had talked with Al Saoub approximately two weeks prior to that interview. . . . Al Saoub never stated where he was calling from and would never say much during the telephone conversations because Al Saoub was afraid that Benziadi's telephone was being monitored by the Federal Bureau of Investigation."

In addition to sending money and e-mails to her former husband, October Lewis also spoke by phone with Battle during his efforts to enter Afghanistan. "Lewis maintained contact with Battle via telephone and e-mail while Battle was out of the country," McCartney affirmed in his affidavit.

Some of the communications between Battle and Lewis might have raised preemptive suspicions had they been reviewed in a timely manner. On Nov. 2, 2001, for example, Battle was in Kashgar, the city on the Chinese side of the mountainous frontier between China, Pakistan and Afghanistan. In an e-mail cited in the prosecutors' sentencing memorandum, he told Lewis of his deep frustration in trying to get over the border. . . .

Battle e-mailed Lewis again on Nov. 12, 2001, this time from Beijing, where he had unsuccessfully tried to secure a visa for Pakistan. "Baby this what I'm about to tell you is for your information only. It is not for you to inform anybody of this at all," wrote Battle. . . .

The Patriot Act . . . definitely gets credit for helping to bring the case to a successful conclusion.

On Nov. 14, 2001, Lewis e-mailed back: ". . . So what do you want me to tell the brother if he ask about you?"

Six days later, Battle replied from Bangladesh. He was obviously worried that his telephone calls back to the United States might be intercepted. . . . His communications, as well as communications involving other Portland cell members as they traveled through Asia, are a perfect fit for the criteria that Gen. Michael Hayden, deputy director of national intelligence, has said are used in the NSA intercept program ordered by President Bush: They were international communications in and out of the U.S. in which there was a reasonable basis to believe one party was linked to al Qaeda.

So did the NSA discover the Portland Seven through intercepts? Apparently not. In a January 17 front-page story that deprecated the effectiveness of the NSA program, the *New York Times* cited the Portland Seven as one case that actually "might have" been assisted by NSA intercepts. But U.S. District Judge Mike Mosman, who had served as the Portland-based U.S. attorney who oversaw the prosecution of the Portland Seven, says otherwise. When I asked Judge Mosman if NSA intercepts were in any way involved in the case, he said, "I first heard about NSA intercepts in mid-December when I read it in the *New York Times*."

The judge pointed to a more conventional genesis for the investigation. "It began with a tip from a deputy sheriff from Skamania County," he said.

Skamania County is in Southern Washington State. The event there to which Judge Mosman referred occurred Sept. 29, 2001, a few weeks before the members of the Portland cell departed for China. Deputy Sheriff Mark Mercer, answering a call from a nearby resident who heard gunfire, came across a group of men shooting guns in a fenced and gated gravel pit. Some of the men wore turbans. Four of them, including Battle, Ford and Al Saoub, were later discovered to be members of the Portland terror cell. Another was Ali Khalid Steitiye . . .

In his 2004 plea agreement, Steitiye conceded that: "While at the gravel pit, defendant Ali Khalid Steitiye made the machine gun available for firing by Habes Al Saoub (aka Abu Tarek) and other members of the group, knowing that they intended to travel to Afghanistan to join the Taliban in violent jihad in the wake of the events at the World Trade Center and Pentagon on Sept. 11, 2001."

"Good Police Work"

Deputy Mercer, of course, had no way of knowing these men were practicing to kill Americans in Afghanistan. He told them to put down their guns, wrote down their names and let them go. At the direction of his boss, then-Sheriff Charles Bryan, he reported the incident to the FBI. In December 2001, when Bryan saw a news report that Steitiye had been arrested on gun charges, he recognized the name and reminded the FBI of the deputy's report.

"It was just good police work," Bryan told the *Seattle Post-Intelligencer* a year later, after members of the Portland Seven were arrested. "I'm proud of how [Mercer] handled it at the time. Now that I think about it, I'm glad he was safe when he went out on the call.". . .

If the National Security Agency must bow to a local deputy sheriff on the question of who started the investigation that nabbed the Portland Seven, the Patriot Act—which was debated in the weeks immediately after 9/11 and signed into law on Oct. 26, 2001—definitely gets credit for helping to bring the case to a successful conclusion.

At least some of the defendants in the Portland Seven case were aware of the broad outlines of the Patriot Act— and complained that it crimped their terrorist plans.

"Two changes in the law made by the Patriot Act were helpful to the investigation and prosecution of the Portland Seven," says Assistant U.S. Attorney Gorder.

The first change was the one that tore down the "wall" that formerly prevented federal investigators collecting intelligence information under a Foreign Intelligence Surveillance Act warrant from sharing that information with federal investigators conducting a criminal investigation. Gorder explains how this change factored into federal prosecutors' calculations in dealing with Jeffrey Leon Battle's confession to a government informant that his group had considered attacking Jewish schools and synagogues.

"By the time our informant recorded this statement from Battle," said Gorder, "we had information that a number of other persons besides Battle had been involved in the Afghanistan conspiracy. Several of these other individuals had returned to the United States, but we did not have sufficient evidence to arrest them."

Battle specifically invoked President Bush's name in reflecting on his own failure as a terrorist.

"Pre-Patriot Act, we faced a dilemma," said Gorder. "Should we arrest Battle immediately to make sure that he didn't now carry out a domestic attack? If so, the other suspects would undoubtedly scatter or attempt to cover up their crimes. The intelligence side of the FBI could still conduct surveillance of Battle, but pre-Patriot Act they were forbidden to communicate what they learned with prosecutors and their own criminal investigators. With the intelligence-sharing changes of the Patriot Act, the FBI was able to conduct FISA surveillance of Battle to detect whether he received orders from some international terrorist group to reinstate the domestic attack plan on Jewish targets and keep us informed as to what they were learning. This gave us the confidence not to prematurely arrest Battle while we continued to gather evidence on the others. Ultimately, we were able to file charges on six defendants, and later a seventh," said Gorder. "Without these changes in the Patriot Act, our case would have been the 'Portland One' rather than the Portland Seven."

Another provision of the Patriot Act that the prosecutors found helpful was Section 220, which allows a judge in a jurisdiction where a crime is committed to issue a search warrant for an e-mail account even if the Internet Service Provider is in another jurisdiction. In the case of the Portland Seven, Gorder said, "[U]nder the old law an agent would have been required to spend taxpayer money to fly to New York and California to obtain a search warrant, rather than go to see a judge here in Portland."

"Everybody's Scared"

Finally, there is the psychological impact the high-profile Patriot Act had on Jeffrey Leon Battle and others who were involved—or who might have become involved—in a conspiracy to wage war against America.

"As an aside, you might be intrigued to know that at least some of the defendants in the Portland Seven case were aware of the broad outlines of the Patriot Act—and complained that it crimped their terrorist plans," said Gorder. "Jeffrey Battle explained why his group eventually failed in their mission to get to Afghanistan—because their plan was not sufficiently organized, in part due to the Patriot Act."

Although laws prohibiting material support for terrorists existed before the Patriot Act, the Patriot Act made them better.

In fact, Battle specifically invoked President Bush's name in reflecting on his own failure as a terrorist. He once told an informant: "[T]he reason it was not organized is, couldn't be organized as it should've been, is because we don't have support. Everybody's scared to give up any money to help us. You know what I'm saying? Because of the law that Bush wrote about, you know, supporting terrorism whatever the whole thing. . . . Everybody's scared . . . [Bush] made a law that say, for instance, I left out of the country and I fought, right, but I wasn't able to afford a ticket but you bought my plane ticket, you gave me the money to do it . . . By me going and me fighting and doing that they can, by this new law, they can come and take you and put you in jail for supporting what they call terrorism."

Gorder notes that although laws prohibiting material support for terrorists existed before the Patriot Act, the Patriot Act made them better. "Battle's overall legal analysis was correct," says Gorder, "if one provides material support such as a plane ticket for terrorist activity or a designated foreign terrorist organization, one can be prosecuted. Although these material support statutes existed before the Patriot Act, the Patriot Act made a number of changes to increase the penalties and make those statutes workable."

If the Patriot Act is allowed to sunset, the impact it had on the plans of people like Jeffrey Leon Battle will sunset, too.

The question for lawmakers in Washington, D.C. is simple: Do they want to keep in place all the redundant layers of protection that stand between us and the next 9/11?

Finally, court documents point to another element that played a role in catching the Portland Seven: good, old-fashioned, nosy neighbors. When Squad of Death leader Habis al Soub was preparing to depart for China in October 2001, for example, he deposited a plastic grocery bag in a recycling bin at his apartment complex. A neighbor fished out the bag, which held a Jordanian passport and an Islamic "martyr's will," and turned it over to the FBI.

The ultimate lesson here may be that redundancy worked in catching the Portland Seven. Even though NSA intercepts were not involved in this case, NSA surveillance might in fact, in a similar future case, pick up exactly the sort of international communications the Portland Seven made. The Patriot Act was crucial in Portland in allowing the use of wiretaps to prevent a potential attack within the United States while giving authorities the opportunity to round up as many co-conspirators as possible. A local sheriff reported key information to the FBI. And alert neighbors helped protect their community against a very real threat.

The question for lawmakers in Washington, D.C. is simple: Do they want to keep in place all the redundant layers of protection that stand between us and the next 9/11? Or do they want to strip one or more of them away?

The Patriot Act Does Not Contain Enough Safeguards Against Mistakes

Bob Barr

Bob Barr is the chairman of a network of conservative organizations called Patriots to Restore Checks and Balances. He is a former member of the U.S. House of Representatives.

We strongly urge Congress to resist calls to summarily remove the sunset provisions in the PATRIOT Act. This reflects our philosophy in support of all necessary and constitutional powers with which to fight acts of terrorism, but against the centralization of undue authority in any one arm or agency of government.

As I have said many times before, I believe the current struggle to properly integrate our shared constitutional heritage into our efforts to provide for the common defense is the defining debate of our time. If we fail to strike the appropriate balance, we will do irreparable harm to our most elemental principles as a nation....

Even though I voted for the USA PATRIOT Act in October 2001, as did many of my colleagues, I did so with the understanding it was an extraordinary measure for an extraordinary threat; that it would be used exclusively, or at least primarily, in the context of important anti-terrorism cases; and that the Department of Justice would be cautious in its implementation and forthcoming in providing information on its use to the Congress and the American people.

I have become skeptical on all of these fronts.

Bob Barr, testimony before the Select Committee on Intelligence, U.S. Senate, April 19, 2005.

Grounds for Skepticism

First, the Justice Department has been quite frank in its use and desire to use the USA PATRIOT Act in *non-terrorism* contexts. Second, the administration has repeatedly stated its intention to expand the USA PATRIOT Act, and has floated various pieces of legislation that would do so.

The USA PATRIOT Act, by lessening meaningful judicial oversight, reduces the ability of the FBI and Justice Department to avoid [honest] mistakes.

And, third, although this Committee would be in the best position to judge, the Justice Department has not produced any compelling evidence that the USA PATRIOT Act has been essential in preventing al Qaeda-style terrorist plots. Although I grant we have not suffered another major terrorist attack since 9-11, as Homeland Security Secretary Michael Chertoff put it, "[i]t's like sprinkling powder to keep away elephants. If no elephants show up, how do you prove it's because of the powder, rather than because there were never any elephants?"

There need be no malice aforethought for something to constitute an "abuse."

Before I specifically discuss those provisions of the USA PATRIOT Act most pertinent to this Committee's jurisdiction, I would like to bring two new developments in the "sunsets" debate to the Committee's attention. Namely, we learned earlier this month both that the USA PATRIOT Act appears to have been used in the Brandon Mayfield affair, and that the Administration is increasingly turning to it for its surveillance needs.

The Mayfield Affair

The Mayfield revelation is particularly disturbing. Mayfield—the Oregon lawyer turned prime suspect in the Madrid bombing investigation because of faulty fingerprint analysis at the FBI—was subjected to a highly intrusive federal investigation and then detained as a "material witness" for two weeks before finally being exonerated.

According to Attorney General Gonzales, the FBI used the USA PATRIOT Act when it executed a covert search of Mayfield's home. Specifically, the attorney general said that Section 207 was used to extend the duration of Mayfield's surveillance, and that "in some sense" Section 218, which made it easier to use intelligence authorities in criminal contexts, was used.

We all fully understand the FBI is not perfect and generally support the bureau even when it makes honest mistakes.

However, the Mayfield case shows how the USA PATRIOT Act, by lessening meaningful judicial oversight, reduces the ability of the FBI and Justice Department to avoid such mistakes. In particular, it shows how—through the increased use of classified and less exacting foreign intelligence surveillance authority in place of traditional criminal warrants based on probable cause and executed in the open—the USA PATRIOT Act can compound mistakes and amplify them into serious deprivations of an innocent person's personal liberty.

In Mayfield's case, not only was a U.S. citizen detained, but his home was subjected to a "black bag" intelligence search even though the Justice Department was arguably conducting this search primarily for criminal purposes; in other words, in order to apprehend a suspect in a terrorist bombing that had already taken place. Such a foreign intelligence search is even more intrusive than the criminal "sneak and peek" search warrants available under section 213 of the USA PATRIOT Act, because notice is not simply delayed, it is never provided. The *Washington Post* reported that in a March 24th letter to Mayfield, the Justice Department acknowledged that during a covert search of his home, agents copied computer and paper files, took 355 digital photographs, seized six cigarette butts for DNA analysis, and used cotton swabs to obtain other DNA evidence.

Overbroad laws are necessarily subject to overbroad application, if not now, then under future administrations.

In short, the Mayfield case should serve as a cautionary tale of how the USA PATRIOT Act can seriously exacerbate any "broken telephone" effect in an ongoing investigation.

Patriot Act Abuses

I would also say, especially to Senators [Orrin] Hatch and [Dianne] Feinstein, that this is the type of problem that supporters of increased checks and balances refer to when discussing so-called "PATRIOT Act abuses." No one is of the mind that the FBI would deliberately seek to infringe on the rights of loyal, law-abiding Americans. But there need be no malice aforethought for something to constitute an "abuse." The fact is, procedural deficiencies in the law's implementation likely led to Mayfield's predicament, and Mayfield was an innocent man.

Put another way, sometimes the road to abuse is paved with good intentions. Take, for instance, the Racketeer Influenced and Corrupt Organizations, or RICO, Act, which was passed to provide tools to fight organized crime, but was then used against pro-life groups. Overbroad laws are necessarily subject to overbroad application, if not now, then under future administrations, including those with less regard for civil liberties. That in itself can be deemed "abusive."

The second consideration—that the USA PATRIOT Act is becoming an ever more popular tool for the Justice Department—should be of particular concern to limited government conservatives like myself. As with taxes, unduly expanded government authority is next to impossible to retract.

Given the reach of the statute, the increased enthusiasm for its use ought to sound alarms.

Increased Use of the PATRIOT Act

As an illustration, I would point the Committee to the attorney general's statement that, to date, Section 215 of the USA PATRIOT Act has been used 35 times. Note, however, that former Attorney General John Ashcroft declassified a memorandum to FBI Director Robert Mueller in September 2003 saying that Section 215 had *never* been used, meaning that those 35 court orders have all been issued in just the last year-and-a-half.

Granted, three dozen court orders may be considered by some to be a drop in the ocean of foreign intelligence document-production orders. Clearly, however, the trend is toward increased, not decreased, use of the USA PATRIOT Act; and, given the reach of the statute, the increased enthusiasm for its use ought to sound alarms.

Similarly, on the eve of the April 6th Senate Judiciary Committee hearing, the Justice Department released statistics disclosing the use to date of Section 213 of the PATRIOT Act—the so-called "sneak and peek" provision that grants statutory authorization for the indefinite delay of criminal search warrant notification.

Apparently, the department sought and received the authority to delay notice 108 times between April 2003 and January 2005, a period of approximately 22 months. By contrast, it sought and received this authority 47 times between November 2001, when the PATRIOT Act was enacted, and April 2003, a period of about 17 months. The five-month difference in timeframe aside, these numbers clearly reveal a substantial increase in use.

Moreover, Senator Arlen Specter at the April 6th Judiciary Committee hearing also revealed that 92—or approximately 60 percent—of those 155 requests were granted under the broad justification that notice would have the result of "seriously jeopardizing an investigation," rather than under the more specific criteria that notice would endanger a person's life, imperil evidence, induce flight from prosecution or lead to witness tampering.

Broadening of Criminal Investigative Powers

While I understand the jurisdiction of this Committee is concerned primarily with foreign intelligence authorities, not with criminal "sneak and peek" warrants, I respectfully submit that you should be concerned when criminal investigative powers are made so broad that they come to resemble powers associated with foreign intelligence investigations. As Attorney General Gonzales informed Representative Flake at an April 7th hearing of the House Judiciary Committee, six criminal delayed-notice warrants under section 213 of the PATRIOT Act were approved with an *indefinite* delay (just as we had feared), and one had a delay that lasted fully half a year.

Lengthy, secret surveillance, including secret "black bag" jobs (all undertaken, since 1978, with the proper approval of the Foreign Intelligence Surveillance Court, of course) have long been the hallmark of a specialized, but crucial, type of investigation—the foreign intelligence investigation of suspected spies and international terrorists—the members of this Committee understand better than anyone. When these intrusive powers, such as the power to enter a home without notifying the owner, become more common in criminal or other types of investigations, the American people become alarmed. The resulting furor risks more draconian limits on all such secret surveillance powers—even in the investigations where they may actually be needed.

Although I acknowledge the Justice Department's argument that Section 213 and 215 searches and surveillance represent only a fraction of the searches and surveillance conducted by the FBI and other security agencies, I remain concerned. These are extraordinary authorities and they are being used more frequently, and more and more outside their proper context of foreign intelligence and terrorism investigations. Any hint of such a trend should be very worrisome.

Increasing Use of Wiretaps

Furthermore, I would point the committee's attention to an April 1, 2005 Associated Press story on a recent report to Congress by the Assistant Attorney General for Legislative Affairs, William E. Moschella, disclosing the record number of Foreign Intelligence Surveillance Act, or FISA, wiretaps in 2004. The department requested and won approval of 1,754 FISA wiretaps in 2004, up from 1,724 in 2003.

A number of provisions in the law made ... wiretaps more intrusive and much easier to obtain outside of terrorism or espionage investigations.

Although the marginal increase between 2003 and 2004 is small, the numbers still represent a 70 percent jump over the number obtained in 2000. In 2003, moreover, the use of intelligence wiretaps outstripped that of normal criminal wiretaps for the first time in history. One can only presume that the same trend continued in 2004.

The USA PATRIOT Act is directly relevant to the increased use of these intelligence wiretaps, as a number of provisions in the law made these wiretaps more intrusive and much easier to obtain outside of terrorism or espionage investigations. Section 218, for instance, which is set to sunset this year, now requires the investigation of foreign intelligence or terrorism to be a "significant purpose," rather than the primary purpose, of the intelligence wiretap. . . .

Roving Wiretaps Can Be Abused

When Congress created foreign intelligence roving wiretap authority in the USA PATRIOT Act, it failed to include the checks against abuse present in the analogous criminal statute. This is troubling because, as roving wiretaps attach to the target of the surveillance and not to the individual communications device, they provide a far more extensive and intrusive record of a person's communications.

Accordingly, criminal roving wiretaps require agents to "ascertain" that the target, rather than a third-party, is in fact using the telephone before they begin recording. They also require that, if the FBI does not actually know the identity (or an alias) of the target, but knows that he or she will be using a particular phone, the wiretap can attach to a single phone and all its users.

In creating roving wiretap authority under FISA, the USA PATRIOT Act did away with this ascertainment requirement. Then, shortly thereafter, the intelligence authorization bill for FY2002 took away the requirement that the applicant specify either the identity of the target *or* the particular communications device.

The result, today [April 19, 2005], is a "John Doe" general warrant, issued secretly under FISA, that permits electronic surveillance irrespective of the communications device being tapped *or* the person being eavesdropped on.

The Justice Department has defended the open-ended nature of these "John Doe" wiretaps, by pointing to the requirement that the FBI provide the FISA court with a physical description of the target if it cannot identify the communications device or target. Critics question how much of a safeguard this description requirement is in practice, given the paucity of identifying information it requires. In recognition of the oversight authority and security clearance of this Committee, I would urge its members to inquire on this point at length.

In addition, I would urge the Committee to tighten the roving wiretap authority to prevent anonymous or dragnet wiretapping, and to use the internal safeguards in the criminal roving wiretap statute as a model. At the very least, a judge authorizing a roving wiretap should have some assurance that (a) an innocent bystander's sensitive communications are protected, and (b) the court order is not an effective *general warrant* to be filled in later. . . .

Risk to Constitutional Freedoms

As evidenced by the circumstances surrounding the founding of this very Committee, foreign intelligence law, especially as it applies domestically, poses serious risks to basic constitutional freedoms. While some hail the provisions in the USA PATRIOT Act as breaking down an artificial "wall" or a "technicality" between the gathering and use of evidence in criminal cases—matters necessarily subject to the Bill of Rights—and the gathering of foreign intelligences—appropriately *not* subject in its gathering to the limitations in the Bill of Rights—the fact is the artificial "wall" that applied different standards to the gathering and use of each category of information, is neither artificial nor a technicality: it is the Constitution of the United States of America. In treating them as one and the same in the name of fighting "terrorism" or any other threat posed to the good order and safety of our society, we show disdain for the fundamental underpinning of our constitutional form of government and the freedoms it enshrines.

Doing otherwise will result in an historical pattern where such laws are made ever more secret, ever more unchecked and ever more susceptible to abuse; and each subsequent national "crisis" forces the shades drawn tighter. It is a slippery slope, down which this Committee, this year in consideration of whether to sunset certain provisions in the USA PATRIOT Act and in deciding whether to place very modest and limited—but fundamentally important—restraints on some of the law's provisions, can help avoid.

The Patriot Act Should Be Amended to Respect Fourth Amendment Rights

Anita Ramasastry

Anita Ramasastry is an associate professor of law at the University of Washington School of Law and a director of the Shidler Center for Law, Commerce & Technology.

On December 31, [2005,] sixteen portions of the USA Patriot Act are set to expire—or in legal parlance, "sunset." Currently, Congress is holding hearings on the Act. It is considering, among other issues, whether to amend it to curb the broad surveillance powers the Act bestowed on the federal government.

For example, under the Act, the government can now monitor an individual's web surfing records. It can use roving wiretaps to monitor phone calls made by individuals "proximate" to the primary person being tapped. It can access Internet Service Provider records. And it can even monitor the private records of people involved in legitimate protests.

After September 11, 2001, when the Act was passed, the Executive argued that these broader powers would be used to put terrorists behind bars. In fact, several of the Act's provisions can be used to gain information about Americans in the context of investigations *with no demonstrated link to terrorism.*

For this reason, I will argue, the Act should be amended. The USA Patriot Act as a whole includes important powers. But as written, the Act goes far beyond its justification: terrorism prevention.

Anita Ramasastry, "The Important But Flawed USA Patriot Act," Findlaw.com, April 20, 2005. Reproduced by permission.

In this column, I will focus on just a few of the Act's sunsetting provisions—each of which, in my view, should be repealed or, at a minimum, allowed to expire [in] December [2005]....

The Burden of Proof

Before I consider these sunsetting sections of the Act, I will first consider what burden of proof should apply, and what information is available to help us evaluate the Act's use.

In its final report, the 9/11 Commission recommended that President Bush should bear the burden of proof to show that Congress ought to renew the Act provisions that are subject to "sunset" limitations. Specifically, the Commission recommended that the provisions be allowed to sunset unless the President can show that each power actually materially enhances security, and that there is adequate supervision of the use of such powers to ensure that civil liberties are protected.

In many cases, based on the information that has so far been made public, it is clear that such a showing cannot be made. Moreover, the Executive Branch should make more information public before Congress decides.

The FBI and the Department of Homeland Security have provided anecdotal information about the law's use, but some politicians have rightfully grown frustrated with the lack of detailed information.

The USA Patriot Act blurred the key contrasts between foreign-intelligence-gathering and domestic law enforcement.

For instance, Senator Jon Kyl (AZ-R) has released a file indicating that requests to the Justice Department "to provide a comprehensive report" on the "provisions of the Patriot Act subject to 'sunset' remain unfulfilled." However, as Kyl's file adds, "Such a report is a critical element in [Congress'] responsibility to provide meaningful oversight before determining whether to change the law with respect to these provisions."

The Department of Justice should provide Congress with full accountings of how the government has used its new-found authority under the Patriot Act. But as I will explain, even the information we have so far provides reason enough to cause Congress to either allow these sections to "sunset," or, at a minimum, significantly amend them.

Pre-Patriot Act Surveillance Regime Respected Fourth Amendment Rights

Our legal system has long separated foreign-intelligence-gathering from domestic criminal enforcement. But under the USA Patriot Act, the distinction is significantly blurred.

Before discussing that blurring, though, it's worth noting how clear the distinction was *before* the USA Patriot Act was enacted into law. At that time, the law struck a fine constitutional balance when it came to electronic surveillance. Since then, that balance has been destroyed.

In 1978, the FISA (Foreign Intelligence Surveillance Act) established a court—known as the FISA Court—with power to issue secret warrants. The purpose of these warrants was to aid in intelligence-gathering, with a view toward preventing espionage and terrorism.

The result [of the Patriot Act] is to open the door to an end run around Americans' Fourth Amendment rights.

Thus, the statute made clear that "the purpose" of FISA-warrant-authorized surveillance would be solely to gather foreign intelligence. And to procure such a warrant, the government had to convince the FISA court there was "probable cause" that the surveillance target was a foreign power or an agent of a foreign power.

The contrast between this standard, and the standard applicable in federal domestic criminal cases was stark. Under the Fourth Amendment, in federal domestic criminal cases, a warrant to intercept a communication or a search warrant must be based on "probable cause" *to believe that a crime has been or is being committed.* If a prosecutor could convince a federal judge that such probable cause existed, a warrant would be issued in a domestic federal criminal case.

The contrast between FISA surveillance and surveillance in regular criminal investigations is stark too. First, there is the secrecy: The targets of FISA surveillance are never notified that they were spied on. In contrast, a domestic criminal defendant gets a copy of the warrant so that he can challenge its legality under the Fourth Amendment, contending that because "probable cause" was lacking, the fruit of the search should not be admitted as evidence in federal court.

Second, there is the lack of clear precedent. The FISA court does not publish its decisions and procedures, as other federal courts do. So unlike in other federal courts, in the FISA court, there is no way for defendants and their attorneys to know how the court interprets the legal standards it applies. Nor is there a way for them to argue that the courts is departing from its own, or a higher court's, binding precedents—an important litigation tactic for federal criminal defense attorneys.

Third, and finally, there is the lack of recourse. There is no clear way to challenge FISA-authorized surveillance—the court doesn't even have a public address. In contrast, federal criminal defendants, again, may move to suppress the evidence that results from a warrant that is not supported by "probable cause."

The Patriot Act Should Be Amended

The USA Patriot Act blurred the key contrasts between foreign-intelligence-gathering and domestic law enforcement.

Now, intelligence-gathering need *not* be the sole purpose of FISA-warrant-authorized surveillance.

Instead, as a result of Section 218 of the PATRIOT Act, intelligence gathering need only be "a significant purpose" of FISA-authorized surveillance.

The result has been that not just CIA agents, but FBI agents as well—or even state police, cooperating with the CIA and FBI—have the ability to utilize FISA's secrecy and lower legal standards. No longer must they prove "probable cause" that a crime has been, or is being, committed—as the Fourth Amendment requires. Instead, all they have to prove is that foreign intelligence is a "significant" purpose of the surveillance. Another purpose can be domestic law enforcement....

The result is to open the door to an end run around Americans' Fourth Amendment rights. Unable even to see the basis for the secret FISA warrant that authorized a search of their home or business, Americans may not be able to challenge that warrant in a criminal proceeding.

Given that FISA warrants allow federal agents to avoid Fourth Amendment challenges, it's no surprise that they are being used more and more frequently. Indeed, some data indicates that there is now more surveillance being authorized by the FISA court, than by all the other federal courts, in the fifty states, combined.

Clearly, the new "significant purpose" standard is problematic. Granted, there may be some circumstances in which domestic criminal investigations are genuinely connected to foreign intelligence, so that the "sole purpose" standard is too limiting for law enforcement.

For instance, suppose that an investigation focused on surveillance of spies also uncovers a domestic plot by Americans to forge pilot's licenses in service of domestic terrorism—in a sort of September-11-meets-Oklahoma-City scenario. In that kind of situation, it could be appropriate for a FISA warrant to cover the whole investigation, even though "foreign intelligence" was not its sole purpose.

But these situations are few and far between. Even if the "sole purpose" standard is not reinstated, the "significant purpose" standard should be clearly limited by the requirement of a nexus to terrorism on the domestic side. The FISA Review Court, in a historic first decision, previously stated that "the FISA process cannot be used as a device to investigate *wholly unrelated* ordinary crimes." As I asked before, however, what about loosely related ordinary crimes? Will law enforcement be able to bypass the Fourth Amendment when it comes to them, too?

Also, it might be possible that for terroristic crimes, even those with no connection to foreign intelligence, Fourth Amendment standards should be different. But that is a question for the courts, not for Congress, to answer.

Roving Wiretaps Should Have Sensible Privacy Safeguards

Gregory T. Nojeim and Timothy H. Edgar

Gregory T. Nojeim is the associate director and chief legislative counsel of the American Civil Liberties Union. Timothy H. Edgar is its national security policy counsel.

It is a pleasure to testify before you on behalf of the American Civil Liberties Union at this oversight hearing on two sections of the USA Patriot Act—section 215, a provision allowing the government to obtain library, bookstore and other personal records in foreign intelligence cases without individual suspicion, and section 206, the provision authorizing roving wiretaps in foreign intelligence cases.

The Patriot Act became law only 45 days after the September 11 [2001] attacks. While it acted swiftly, Congress subjected approximately a dozen provisions of the Patriot Act to a sunset date of December 31, 2005, so that it could take a second look at them.

Congress was wise to do so. Terrorism has been with us for a long time. It will likely be with us for generations to come. The decisions that you make over the coming months about the Patriot Act must be made with an eye toward that reality.

Congress should use the debate over the renewal of parts of the Patriot Act as an opportunity to reassert its rightful role in determining law enforcement and national security policy in the post-9/11 context, which has waned as the power of the Executive Branch has waxed. Before re-authorizing any power, this committee should require the Executive Branch to meet the standard articulated by the bipartisan 9-11 Commission.

Gregory T. Nojeim and Timothy H. Edgar, "Testimony before the Subcommittee on Crime, Terrorism and Homeland Security of the Judiciary Committee, U.S. House of Representatives," American Civil Liberties Union (ACLU), April 28, 2005, pp. 1–8. Copyright © 2005 ACLU, 125 Broad Street, 18th Floor, New York, NY 10004. Reproduced by permission.

First, Congress should take care not to renew any provision unless the government can show "(a) that the power actually materially enhances security and (b) that there is adequate supervision of the executive's use of the powers to ensure protection of civil liberties."[1]

Second, "[i]f the power is granted, there must be adequate guidelines and oversight to properly confine its use."[2]

Finally, Congress should resist efforts by the Executive Branch to evade searching review of its existing powers, both under the Patriot Act and under other legal authorities, by shifting the debate to new anti-terrorism legislation, such as proposals for administrative subpoenas.

Congress may not be able to fully review or assess the effectiveness, and impact on civil liberties, of some anti-terrorism powers that the Executive Branch was granted in the Patriot Act. The lack of meaningful information about the use of many powers is sometimes a direct result of excessive secrecy in the Executive Branch, and sometimes the result of necessary secrecy. In any case where sufficient information is not available to undertake a thorough review, Congress should set a new sunset date and impose additional reporting requirements to facilitate a proper review, rather than cede those powers permanently to the Executive Branch. . . .

"Roving Wiretaps" Without Sensible Privacy Safeguards

"General warrants"—blank warrants that do not describe what may be searched—were among those oppressive powers used by the British crown that led directly to the American Revolution. As a result, the framers required all warrants to "particularly describ[e] the place to be searched, and the persons or things to be seized."

1. Final Report of the National Commission on Terrorist Attacks Upon the United States ("The 9/11 Commission Report") 294-95 (2004) (boldfaced recommendation).
2. *Id.*

The same "particularity" requirements apply to wiretap orders. In the landmark case *United States v. Donovan* (1977), a majority upheld the federal criminal wiretap law, noting that Congress had redrafted the law to include safeguards regarding, among other things, the need to identify targets of surveillance in response to the "constitutional command of particularization."[3]

Section 206 of the Patriot Act erodes the basic constitutional rule of particularization by creating "roving wiretaps" in foreign intelligence cases without sensible privacy safeguards. As amended by later legislation, these wiretaps do more than allow the government to get a single order that follows the target of surveillance from telephone to telephone. The government can now issue "John Doe" roving wiretaps that fail to specify a target or a telephone, and can use wiretaps without checking that the conversations they are intercepting actually involve a target of the investigation. Section 206 is subject to the Patriot Act's sunset clause.

When Congress enacted roving wiretaps for criminal investigations, it insisted on important privacy safeguards.

Prior to the passage of the Patriot Act, roving wiretaps were available in criminal investigations (including criminal investigations of terrorists), but were not available in foreign intelligence investigations.

Because roving wiretaps contain more potential for abuse than traditional wiretaps, which apply to a single telephone or other device, when Congress enacted roving wiretaps for criminal investigations, it insisted on important privacy safeguards.

First, a criminal wiretap must specify either the identity of the target or the communications device being used. In other

---

3. *Id.* at 426-27 (quoting S. Rep. No. 1097, 90th Cong., 2nd Sess., at 66 (1968), *reprinted in* U.S. Code Cong. and Admin. News 1968 at 2190).

words, a surveillance order may specify only the target, or only the phone, but it must specify one or the other. Second, a criminal wiretap that jumps from phone to phone or other device may not be used unless the government "ascertains" that the target identified by the order is actually using that device.

A roving tap, unbounded by any need to identify the target, opens the door to surveillance of . . . anyone else who might be using that telephone.

When Congress enacted the Patriot Act, it extended "roving wiretap" authority to FISA investigations, but did not include the common sense "ascertainment" safeguard. Shortly thereafter, the newly enacted roving wiretap authority was broadened by the Intelligence Act for FY 2002, which authorized wiretaps where neither the target nor the device was specified. As a result, FISA now allows "John Doe" roving wiretaps. These are new wiretaps that can follow an unknown suspect from telephone to telephone based only on a potentially vague physical description.

The Justice Department points to the need to provide a physical description, and the need to show "probable cause" that the wiretap will intercept conversations of an agent of a foreign power, as sufficient protection for roving surveillance. Congress provided more exacting scrutiny for criminal roving wiretaps, and it should provide additional safeguards here. A roving tap, unbounded by any need to identify the target, opens the door to surveillance of anyone who fits that description, or (because of the lack of an ascertainment requirement) anyone else who might be using that telephone.

Of course, particularization is a separate constitutional demand; probable cause does not satisfy the Fourth Amendment without particularization. For that reason, the criminal roving wiretap statute includes the requirement to identify a target even though criminal wiretap orders also require criminal probable cause. FISA wiretaps, of course, require no probable cause of crime, so the need for safeguards is, if anything, greater.

In its defense of section 206 of the Patriot Act, the Justice Department takes issue with both the ascertainment requirement and the requirement to identify the target of a roving wiretap. The Justice Department's "sunsets report" implies, wrongly, that the ascertainment requirement only applies to oral interceptions (i.e., bugs) and not to wiretaps.[4] While the wording of the ascertainment requirement for wiretaps is different than the same requirement for oral interception,[5] there is no doubt that the criminal wiretap statute bans "John Doe" roving wiretaps and requires ascertainment.

[The Law] which applies to wire and electronic communication, plainly provides that no judge may issue a roving wiretap unless, among other things:

> the application identifies the person believed to be committing the offense and whose communications are to be intercepted and . . . the order authorizing or approving the interception is limited to interception only for such time as it is reasonable to presume that the person identified in the application is or was reasonably proximate to the instrument through which such communication will be or was transmitted.

Congress should tighten the FISA roving wiretap so that it has the sensible safeguards for privacy, just as criminal roving wiretaps. Indeed, FISA roving wiretaps appear to be far more common than criminal roving wiretaps. Attorney General Gonzales reported in testimony before the House Judiciary Committee on April 6, 2005 that FISA roving wiretaps had been issued 49 times since passage of the Patriot Act. By contrast, the federal government reported only six federal crimi-

4. Department of Justice, *USA PATRIOT Act: Sunsets Report* (April 2005, at 20.
5. *See* 18 U.S.C. § 2518(12) (ascertainment requirement for oral interception).

nal roving wiretaps in 2003 (the latest report available), with nine federal criminal roving wiretaps in 2002.[6]

Supporters of the Patriot Act often argue that changes to the law were needed to give the government the same powers in foreign intelligence investigations that it already had in criminal investigations. To the extent that is appropriate, it is fair to insist that the same safeguards apply as well.

We are not asking that law enforcement tools be taken away. Rather, that they be made subject to reasonable checks and balances.

Section 2 of H.R. 1526, the SAFE Act, would provide just such safeguards. While it preserves FISA roving surveillance authority, it also makes sure that these privacy safeguards, which apply to criminal roving wiretaps, would also apply to FISA roving wiretaps.

In short, we are not asking that law enforcement tools be taken away. Rather, that they be made subject to reasonable checks and balances—such as meaningful judicial oversight and appropriate disclosure to the public of use of the power.

6. Wiretap reports are available at the website of the Administrative Office of the U.S. Courts, at http://www.uscourts.gov/library/wiretap.html.

CHAPTER 2

Was National Security Agency (NSA) Wiretapping Without Warrants Legal?

Chapter Preface

In December 2005 a front-page story in the *New York Times* revealed that by executive order of the president, the National Security Agency (NSA) had been secretly conducting surveillance on domestic communications without obtaining search warrants. This activity had been going on since shortly after the terrorist attacks of September 11, 2001. The *Times* had known about it for a year but had delayed publication at the request of the White House, which maintained that exposure could jeopardize future investigations. The program, said reporters James Risen and Eric Lichtblau, was still classified, and they therefore declined to name their sources. These anonymous sources, along with some others involved in the program, were said to have reservations about its legality.

Immediately, the exposé aroused public controversy. There was an outcry from civil libertarians, who held that such surveillance was indeed illegal. By contrast, defenders of the program said it had been "a critical tool in helping disrupt terrorist plots and prevent attacks inside the United States." The Bush administration rushed to elaborate, publicly confirming—to many people's surprise—that the program did exist and explaining that it was limited to situations in which at least one party to the communication was believed to be connected with the terrorist organization Al Qaeda and in which one was outside the United States. Some people doubted this assertion, claming that innocent Americans were being spied on. Later, the dispute expanded to cover other issues.

The role of the NSA historically is to spy on communications abroad; it does not investigate domestic crime, which is dealt with by the FBI. After 9/11, when it became evident that foreign terrorists were operating within the United States, the Patriot Act authorized use of the same surveillance tools for finding suspected terrorists as are used typically for obtaining evidence against criminals. However, such surveillance is subject to the provisions of the Foreign Intelligence Surveillance Act (FISA), which require a search warrant to be obtained from a special secret court, the Foreign Intelligence Surveillance Court (FISC), at the latest within seventy-two hours after such surveillance against a target is begun. The NSA program was bypassing the FISC, most members of which had never been told about it. Was this legal? The president and his supporters argued that it was, because the Constitution gives him the inherent power to act against foreign threats. His opponents were convinced that the FISA limits that power. As is made plain by the viewpoints in this chapter, the debate was carried on at great length.

In January 2007, President Bush agreed to allow the NSA's program to be overseen by the FISC, which issued an order authorizing the government to monitor communications "into or out of the United States where there is probable cause to believe that one of the communicants is a member or agent of Al Qaeda or an associated terrorist organization." But the controversy continued, with the administration maintaining that the FISA is outdated and should be permanently modified to permit more efficient investigation of terrorism (a topic that is covered in Chapter Three of this book).

On September 20, 2007, J. Michael McConnell, the director of national intelligence, told Congress that the ongoing public debate over the Bush administration's warrantless wiretapping program would lead to American deaths by revealing sensitive surveillance methods to potential terrorists. "[Intelligence business] is conducted in secret for a reason," he said. The nation remains divided on the question of whether the greatest danger is from terrorists or from the potential misuse of government domestic surveillance capabilities.

Presidents Can Order Wiretapping for Foreign Intelligence Purposes

John Schmidt

John Schmidt served under President Clinton from 1994 to 1997 as the associate attorney general of the United States. He subsequently was a partner in a Chicago-based law firm.

President Bush's post-Sept. 11, 2001, authorization to the National Security Agency [NSA] to carry out electronic surveillance into private phone calls and e-mails is consistent with court decisions and with the positions of the Justice Department under prior presidents.

The president authorized the NSA program in response to the 9/11 terrorist attacks on America. An identifiable group, Al Qaeda, was responsible and believed to be planning future attacks in the United States. Electronic surveillance of communications to or from those who might plausibly be members of or in contact with Al Qaeda was probably the only means of obtaining information about what its members were planning next. No one except the president and the few officials with access to the NSA program can know how valuable such surveillance has been in protecting the nation.

In the Supreme Court's 1972 Keith decision holding that the president does not have inherent authority to order wiretapping without warrants to combat domestic threats, the court said explicitly that it was not questioning the president's authority to take such action in response to threats from abroad.

John Schmidt, "President Had Legal Authority to OK Taps," *Chicago Tribune*, December 21, 2005. Reproduced by permission of the author.

Four federal courts of appeal subsequently faced the issue squarely and held that the president has inherent authority to authorize wiretapping for foreign intelligence purposes without judicial warrant.

In the most recent judicial statement on the issue, the Foreign Intelligence Surveillance Court of Review, composed of three federal appellate court judges, said in 2002 that "All the . . . courts to have decided the issue held that the president did have inherent authority to conduct warrantless searches to obtain foreign intelligence . . . We take for granted that the president does have that authority."

The passage of the Foreign Intelligence Surveillance Act [FISA] in 1978 did not alter the constitutional situation. That law created the Foreign Intelligence Surveillance Court that can authorize surveillance directed at an "agent of a foreign power," which includes a foreign terrorist group. Thus, Congress put its weight behind the constitutionality of such surveillance in compliance with the law's procedures. But as the 2002 Court of Review noted, if the president has inherent authority to conduct warrantless searches, "FISA could not encroach on the president's constitutional power."

Every President Has Asserted the Power to Go Beyond FISA

Every president since FISA's passage has asserted that he retained inherent power to go beyond the act's terms. Under President Clinton, deputy Atty. Gen. Jamie Gorelick testified that "the Department of Justice believes, and the case law supports, that the president has inherent authority to conduct warrantless physical searches for foreign intelligence purposes."

FISA contains a provision making it illegal to "engage in electronic surveillance under color of law except as authorized by statute." The term "electronic surveillance" is defined to exclude interception outside the U.S., as done by the NSA, unless there is interception of a communication "sent by or intended to be received by a particular, known United States person" (a U.S. citizen or permanent resident) and the communication is intercepted by "intentionally targeting that United States person." The cryptic descriptions of the NSA program leave unclear whether it involves targeting of identified U.S. citizens. If the surveillance is based upon other kinds of evidence, it would fall outside what a FISA court could authorize and also outside the act's prohibition on electronic surveillance.

The administration has offered the further defense that FISA's reference to surveillance "authorized by statute" is satisfied by congressional passage of the post-Sept. 11 resolution giving the president authority to "use all necessary and appropriate force" to prevent those responsible for Sept. 11 from carrying out further attacks. The administration argues that obtaining intelligence is a necessary and expected component of any military or other use of force to prevent enemy action. But even if the NSA activity is "electronic surveillance" and the Sept. 11 resolution is not "statutory authorization" within the meaning of FISA, the act still cannot, in the words of the 2002 Court of Review decision, "encroach upon the president's constitutional power."

FISA does not anticipate a post-Sept. 11 situation. What was needed after Sept. 11, according to the president, was surveillance beyond what could be authorized under that kind of individualized case-by-case judgment. It is hard to imagine the Supreme Court second-guessing that presidential judgment.

Should we be afraid of this inherent presidential power? Of course. If surveillance is used only for the purpose of preventing another Sept. 11 type of attack or a similar threat, the harm of interfering with the privacy of people in this country

is minimal and the benefit is immense. The danger is that surveillance will not be used solely for that narrow and extraordinary purpose.

But we cannot eliminate the need for extraordinary action
in the kind of unforeseen circumstances presented by Sept. 11.
I do not believe the Constitution allows Congress to take away
from the president the inherent authority to act in response to
a foreign attack. That inherent power is reason to be careful
about who we elect as president, but it is authority we have
needed in the past and, in the light of history, could well need
again.

Claims Made by Opponents of the NSA Wiretapping Program Are Untrue

U.S. Department of Justice

The U.S. Department of Justice (DOJ) is a Cabinet department in the United States government designed to enforce the law and defend the interests of the United States. It is administered by the U.S. attorney general.

Myth: The NSA program is illegal.

Reality: The President's authority to authorize the terrorist surveillance program is firmly based both in his constitutional authority as Commander-in-Chief, and in the Authorization for Use of Military Force (AUMF) passed by Congress after the September 11 [2001] attacks.

As Commander-in-Chief and Chief Executive, the President has legal authority under the Constitution to authorize the NSA terrorist surveillance program.

- The Constitution makes protecting our Nation from foreign attack the President's most solemn duty and provides him with the legal authority to keep America safe.

- It has long been recognized that the President has inherent authority to conduct warrantless surveillance to gather foreign intelligence even in peacetime. Every federal appellate court to rule on the question has concluded that the President has this authority and that it is consistent with the Constitution.

U.S. Department of Justice, *The NSA Program to Detect and Prevent Terrorist Attacks: Myth v. Reality*, January 27, 2006.

- Since the Civil War, wiretaps aimed at collecting foreign intelligence have been authorized by Presidents, and the authority to conduct warrantless surveillance for foreign intelligence purposes has been consistently cited and used when necessary.

Congress confirmed and supplemented the President's constitutional authority to authorize this program when it passed the AUMF.

- The AUMF authorized the President to use "all necessary and appropriate military force against those nations, organizations, or persons he determines planned, authorized, committed, or aided in the terrorist attacks that occurred on September 11, 2001."

- In its *Hamdi* decision, the Supreme Court ruled that the AUMF also authorizes the "fundamental incident[s] of waging war." The history of warfare makes clear that electronic surveillance of the enemy is a fundamental incident to the use of military force.

Safeguards are in place to protect the civil liberties of ordinary Americans.

A crucial responsibility of the President—charged by the AUMF and the Constitution—is to identify enemies who attacked us, especially if they are in the United States ready to strike against our Nation.

- We are at war, and al Qaeda is not a conventional enemy. Since the September 11 attacks, it has promised again and again to deliver another, even more devastating attack on America. In the meantime, it has killed hundreds of innocent people around the world through large-scale attacks in Indonesia, Madrid, and London.

- Al Qaeda's plans include infiltrating our cities and communities and plotting with affiliates abroad to kill innocent Americans.

- The United States must use every tool available, consistent with the Constitution, to prevent and deter another al Qaeda attack, and the President has indicated his intent to do just that.

The Supreme Court has long held that the Fourth Amendment allows warrantless searches where "special needs, beyond the normal need for law enforcement," exist.

Myth: The NSA program is a domestic eavesdropping program used to spy on innocent Americans.

Reality: The NSA program is narrowly focused, aimed only at international calls and targeted at al Qaeda and related groups. Safeguards are in place to protect the civil liberties of ordinary Americans.

- The program only applies to communications where one party is located outside of the United States.

- The NSA terrorist surveillance program described by the President is only focused on members of Al Qaeda and affiliated groups. Communications are only intercepted if there is a reasonable basis to believe that one party to the communication is a member of al Qaeda, affiliated with al Qaeda, or a member of an organization affiliated with al Qaeda.

- The program is designed to target a key tactic of al Qaeda: infiltrating foreign agents into the United States and controlling their movements through electronic communications, just as it did leading up to the September 11 attacks.

- The NSA activities are reviewed and reauthorized approximately every 45 days. In addition, the General Counsel and Inspector General of the NSA monitor the program to ensure that it is operating properly and that civil liberties are protected, and the intelligence agents involved receive extensive training.

Myth: The NSA activities violate the Fourth Amendment.

Reality: The NSA program is consistent with the Constitution's protections of civil liberties, including the protections of the Fourth Amendment.

- The Supreme Court has long held that the Fourth Amendment allows warrantless searches where "special needs, beyond the normal need for law enforcement," exist. Foreign intelligence collection, especially in a time of war when catastrophic attacks have already been launched inside the United States, falls within the special needs context.

- As the Foreign Intelligence Surveillance Court of Review has observed, the nature of the "emergency" posed by al Qaeda "takes the matter out of the realm of ordinary crime control."

- The program easily meets the Court's reasonableness test for whether a warrant is required. The NSA activities described by the President are narrow in scope and aim, and the government has an overwhelming interest in detecting and preventing further catastrophic attacks on American soil.

Myth: The NSA program violates the Foreign Intelligence Surveillance Act (FISA).

Reality: The NSA activities described by the President are consistent with FISA.

- FISA expressly envisions a need for the President to conduct electronic surveillance outside of its provisions when a later statute authorizes that surveillance. The AUMF is such a statute.

- The NSA activities come from the very center of the Commander-in-Chief power, and it would raise serious constitutional issues if FISA were read to allow Congress to interfere with the President's well-recognized, inherent constitutional authority. FISA can and should be read to avoid this.

Myth: The Administration could have used FISA but simply chose not to.

Reality: In the war on terrorism, it is sometimes imperative to detect—reliably, immediately, and without delay—whether an al Qaeda member or affiliate is in contact with someone in the United States. FISA is an extremely valuable tool in the war on terrorism, but it was passed in 1978 and there have been tremendous advances in technology since then.

- The NSA program is an "early warning system" with only one purpose: to detect and prevent the next attack on the United States from foreign agents hiding in our midst. It is a program with a military nature that requires speed and agility.

- The FISA process, by design, moves more slowly. It requires numerous lawyers, the preparation of legal briefs, approval from a Cabinet-level officer, certification from the National Security Advisor or another Senate-confirmed officer, and finally, the approval of an Article III judge. This is a good process for traditional domestic foreign intelligence monitoring, but when even 24 hours can make the difference between success and failure in preventing a terrorist attack, a faster process is needed.

Wall Street Journal, "President Taylor," August 18, 2006. www.opinionjournal.com. Reprinted with permission of *The Wall Street Journal*, Dow Jones & Company. All rights reserved.

Myth: FISA has "emergency authorizations" to allow 72-hour surveillance without a court order that the Administration could easily utilize.

Reality: There is a serious misconception about so-called "emergency authorizations" under FISA, which allow 72 hours of surveillance without a court order. FISA requires the Attorney General to determine in advance that a FISA application for that particular intercept will be fully supported and will be approved by the court before an emergency authorization can be granted, and the review process itself can and does take precious time.

- The Justice Department does not approve emergency authorizations without knowing it will receive court approval within 72 hours.

- To initiate surveillance under a FISA emergency authorization, it is not enough to rely on the best judgment of our intelligence officers alone. Those intelligence officers would have to get the sign-off of lawyers at the NSA that all provisions of FISA have been satisfied, then lawyers in the Department of Justice would have to be similarly satisfied, and finally, the Attorney General would have to be satisfied that the search meets the requirements of FISA. The government would have to be prepared to follow up with a full FISA application within 72 hours.

- A typical FISA application involves a substantial process in its own right: The work of several lawyers; the preparation of a legal brief and supporting declarations; the approval of a Cabinet-level officer; a certification from the National Security Advisor, the Director of the FBI, or another designated Senate-confirmed officer; and, finally the approval of an Article III judge.

- The FISA process makes perfect sense in almost all cases of foreign-intelligence monitoring in the United States. Although technology has changed dramatically since FISA was enacted, FISA remains a vital tool in the war on terrorism—one that we are using to its fullest and will continue to use against al Qaeda and other foreign threats.

- But the terrorist surveillance program operated by the NSA requires maximum speed and agility to achieve early warning, and even a very brief delay may make the difference between success and failure in detecting and preventing the next attack.

Congress Cannot Limit a President's Constitutional Powers

Andrew C. McCarthy

Andrew C. McCarthy is a former federal prosecutor and as of 2008 a senior fellow at the Foundation for the Defense of Democracies.

Washington's scandal *du jour* [of the day] involves a wartime surveillance program President Bush directed the National Security Agency [NSA] to carry out after al-Qaeda killed nearly 3,000 Americans on September 11, 2001. The idea that there is anything truly scandalous about this program is absurd. But the outcry against it is valuable, highlighting as it does the mistaken assumption that criminal-justice solutions are applicable to national-security challenges.

The intelligence community has identified thousands of al-Qaeda operatives and sympathizers throughout the world. After Congress overwhelmingly authorized the use of military force immediately following the 9/11 attacks, the president, as part of the war effort, ordered the NSA to intercept the enemy's international communications, even if those communications went into and out of the United States and thus potentially involved American citizens. According to reports from the *New York Times*, which shamefully publicized leaks of the program's existence in mid-December 2005, as many as 7,000 suspected terrorists overseas are monitored at any one time, as are up to 500 suspects inside the U.S.

Andrew C. McCarthy, "How to 'Connect the Dots,'" *National Review*, January 30, 2006, pp. 37–39. Copyright © 2006 by National Review, Inc., 215 Lexington Avenue, New York, NY 10016. Reproduced by permission.

Different from Rogue Intelligence Operations

As is typical of such wartime operations, the NSA program was classified at the highest level of secret information. It was, nevertheless, completely different from the kind of rogue intelligence operations of which the Nixon era is emblematic (though by no means the only case). The Bush administration internally vetted the program, including at the Justice Department, to confirm its legal footing. It reviewed (and continues to review) the program every 45 days. It briefed the bipartisan leadership of Congress (including the intelligence committees) at least a dozen times. It informed the chief judge of the federal Foreign Intelligence Surveillance Court (FISC), the tribunal that oversees domestic national-security wire-tapping. And it modified the program in mid-2004 in reaction to concerns raised by the chief judge, national-security officials, and government lawyers.

As potential scandal fodder, so unremarkable did the NSA program seem that the Times *sat on the story for a year.*

Far from being a pretextual use of war powers to spy on political opponents and policy dissenters, the NSA program has been dedicated to national security. More to the point, it has saved lives, helping break up at least one al-Qaeda conspiracy to attack New York City and Washington, D.C., in connection with which a plotter named Iyman Faris was sentenced to 20 years' imprisonment.

As potential scandal fodder, so unremarkable did the NSA program seem that the *Times* sat on the story for a year—and a year, it is worth noting, during which it transparently and assiduously sought to exploit any opportunity to discredit the administration and cast it as a mortal threat to civil liberties. The leak was not sprung until the eleventh hour of congressional negotiations over renewal of the Patriot Act—at which point it provided ammunition to those who would gut Patriot's crucial post-9/11 domestic-surveillance powers and simultaneously served as a marketing campaign for *Times* reporter James Risen, who just happened to be on the eve of publishing a book about, among other things, Bush's domestic "spying."

In fact, so obviously appropriate was wartime surveillance of the enemy that Rep. Jane Harman, the ranking Democrat on the House Intelligence Committee, issued a statement right after the *Times* exposed the program, saying: "I have been briefed since 2003 on a highly classified NSA foreign collection program that targeted Al-Qaeda. I believe the program is essential to US national security and that its disclosure has damaged critical intelligence capabilities." (With partisan "scandal" blowing in the wind, Harman changed her tune two weeks later, suddenly deciding that the "essential" program was probably illegal after all.)

A Mighty Fuss

If President Bush's reelection is any indication, what most Americans will care about is that we are monitoring the enemy. Chances are they won't be overly interested in knowing whether that monitoring is done on the president's own constitutional authority or in accordance with a statutory scheme calling for judicial imprimatur. Nevertheless, the Left is already indulging in loose talk about impeachment. Even some Republican "moderates," such as Arlen Specter, say the domestic-spying allegations are troubling enough that hearings are warranted. So it's worth asking: What is all the fuss about?

At bottom, it is about a power grab that began nearly three decades ago. Ever since it became technologically possible to intercept wire communications, presidents have done so. All of them, going back to FDR [Franklin Delano

Roosevelt] claimed that the powers granted to the chief executive under Article II of the Constitution allowed them to conduct such wiretapping for national-security purposes. Particularly in wartime, this power might be thought indisputable. The president is the commander in chief of the armed forces, and penetrating enemy communications is as much an incident of war-fighting as bombing enemy targets is.

But surveillance power has been abused—and notoriously by President [Richard] Nixon, whose eavesdropping on political opponents was the basis of a draft article of impeachment. Watergate-era domestic-spying controversies dovetailed with important developments in the law of electronic surveillance. In 1967, the Supreme Court, in *Katz v. United States*, held that Fourth Amendment protection against unreasonable searches extended to electronic surveillance—meaning that eavesdropping without a judicial warrant was now presumptively unconstitutional. Congress followed by enacting a comprehensive scheme, known as "Title III," that required law-enforcement agents to obtain a court warrant for probable cause of a crime before conducting electronic surveillance. Yet both *Katz* and Title III recognized inherent presidential authority to conduct *national-security* monitoring without being bound by the new warrant requirement.

A constitutional power cannot be altered or limited by statute.

The Supreme Court undertook to circumscribe this inherent authority in its 1972 *Keith* decision. It held that a judicial warrant was required for national-security surveillance if the target was a purely *domestic* threat—the Vietnam-era Court giving higher priority to the free-speech interests of "those suspected of unorthodoxy in their political beliefs" than to the safety of those who might be endangered by domestic terrorists. Still, the Court took pains to exempt from its ruling the "activities of *foreign* powers or their agents" (emphasis added).

Power Grab

The true power grab occurred in 1978, when Congress enacted the Foreign Intelligence Surveillance Act. FISA attempted to do in the national-security realm what Title III had done in law enforcement: erect a thoroughgoing legal regime for domestic eavesdropping. And therein lies the heart of the current dispute. If the president has inherent authority to conduct national-security wiretapping, it is a function of his constitutional warrant. It is not a function of Congress's having failed until 1978 to flex its own muscles. A constitutional power cannot be altered or limited by statute. Period.

But limiting presidential authority is precisely what FISA purports to do. It ostensibly prohibits national-security eavesdropping (and, since 1994, physical searches) unless the executive branch can satisfy a federal judge—one of eleven who sit on a specially created Foreign Intelligence Surveillance Court—that there is probable cause that the subject it seeks to monitor is an "agent of a foreign power" (generally either a spy or a member of a foreign terrorist organization).

FISA does not aim to restrict the power to eavesdrop on *all* conversations. Communications that are entirely foreign—in that they involve aliens communicating overseas, for example—are exempted, as are conversations that *unintentionally* capture "U.S. persons" (generally, American citizens and permanent resident aliens), as long as these communications are intercepted outside the U.S. But where it does apply, FISA holds that the president—the constitutional officer charged with the nation's security—is powerless to eavesdrop on an operative posing a threat to the United States unless a judge—who need not possess any national-security expertise—is persuaded that the operative is a genuine threat. One suspects that such a system would astonish the Founders.

The Bounds of FISA

Does the NSA program violate FISA? That question is difficult to answer with certainty. The program remains highly classified, and many of its details are not publicly known, nor should they be. Much has been made of the fact that FISA approval is required to intercept calls into or out of the United States if an American is intentionally being targeted. But scant attention has been given to FISA's caveat that such conversations are protected only if their participants have a *reasonable expectation of privacy*. It is difficult to imagine that Americans who make or receive calls to war zones in, say, Afghanistan or Iraq, or to al-Qaeda operatives anywhere, can reasonably expect that no one is listening in.

Nevertheless, it would not be surprising to learn that at least some of the NSA monitoring transgresses the bounds of FISA. For example, the statute mandates—without qualification about the reasonable expectation of privacy—that the government seek a judicial warrant before eavesdropping on any international call to or from the U.S., if that call is intercepted *inside* our borders. A distinction based on where a call is intercepted made sense in 1978. Back then, if a conversation was intercepted inside our borders, its participants were almost certain to include at least one U.S. person. But modern technology has since blurred the distinction between foreign and domestic telephony. Packets of digital information are now routed through switches inside countries (including, predominately, the U.S.) where neither the sender nor the recipient of the call is located. The NSA has capitalized on this evolution, and is now able, from within the U.S., to seize calls between Tikrit and Kabul, or between Peshawar and Hamburg. If done without a warrant, those intercepts present no FISA problem, because all the speakers are overseas. But it's hard to believe that the NSA is using this technology *only* to acquire all-foreign calls, while intercepting calls between, say, New York and Hamburg only from locations *outside the* U.S.

Perhaps that is why the Bush administration's defense has been light on the abstruse details of FISA and heavy on the president's inherent Article II power—although carefully couched to avoid offending Congress and the FISC with suggestions that FISA is at least partly unconstitutional. Essentially, the administration argues that FISA is beneficial in ordinary times and for long-term investigations, but that it did not and cannot repeal the president's independent constitutional obligation to protect the country: an obligation that was explicitly reserved even by President Carter, who signed FISA; that has been claimed by every president since; and that is uniquely vital in a war against thousands of stateless, stealthy terrorists, in which both a "probable cause" requirement and a sclerotic bureaucracy for processing warrant applications would be dangerously impractical.

[The Fourth] Amendment proscribes unreasonable searches, not warrantless ones. . . . Plainly, there is nothing unreasonable about intercepting potential enemy communications in wartime.

The Administration's Argument

In advancing this argument, the administration finds much support in the one and only decision ever rendered by the Foreign Intelligence Court of Review—the appellate court created by FISA to review FISC decisions. That decision came in 2002, after a quarter-century of FISA experience. Tellingly, its context was a brazen effort by the FISC to reject the Patriot Act's dismantling of the "wall" that prevented intelligence agents and criminal investigators from pooling information. In overruling the FISC, the Court of Review observed that "all the other courts to have decided the issue [have] held that the President did have inherent authority to conduct warrantless searches to obtain foreign intelligence information." Notwithstanding FISA, the Court thus pronounced: "We take for granted that the President does have that authority."

The administration has also placed great stock in Congress's post-9/11 authorization of "all necessary and appropriate force" against those behind the terrorist attacks. While this resolution did not expressly mention penetrating enemy communications, neither did it explicitly include the detention of enemy combatants, which the Supreme Court, in its 2004 *Hamdi* decision, found implicit in the use-of-force authorization because it is a "fundamental incident of waging war." Capturing intelligence, of course, is as much a component of waging war as capturing operatives. Any other conclusion would lead to the absurdity of the president's having full discretion to kill terrorists but needing a judge's permission merely to eavesdrop on them.

FISA aside, the administration stresses that the NSA program fits comfortably within the Fourth Amendment. That Amendment proscribes *unreasonable* searches, not warrantless ones—and it is thus unsurprising that the Supreme Court has recognized numerous exceptions to the warrant requirement that are of far less moment than the imperative to protect the country from attack. Plainly, there is nothing unreasonable about intercepting potential enemy communications in wartime. Moreover, the courts have long held that searches conducted at the border are part of the sovereign right of self-protection, and thus require neither probable cause nor a warrant. Cross-border communications, which might well be triggers of terror plots, are no more deserving of constitutional protection.

Constitutional Authority

Critics have made much of a lengthy analysis published on January 6, 2006, by the Congressional Research Service that casts doubt on the administration's core contentions. Media have treated the report as bearing special weight because the CRS is a non-partisan entity. But that does not mean the CRS is *objective*. "The sole mission of CRS," it explains on its website, "is to serve the United States Congress." Yet the issue at stake is precisely a separation-of-powers dispute.

The NSA program was a bona fide effort to protect the nation from harm, not to snoop on Americans.

. While the CRS study is an impressive compilation of the relevant law, it resorts to a fairly standard tactic for marginalizing executive power: reliance on the concurring opinion by Supreme Court Justice Robert Jackson in a 1952 case involving President [Harry] Truman's failed effort to seize steel mills—a move Truman justified by referring to the exigencies of the Korean War. Jackson saw executive power as waxing or waning along a three-stage scale, depending on whether a president acted with the support, the indifference, or the opposition of Congress. On this theory, a statute like FISA could curb a president's inherent constitutional authority. The fatal problem with the Jackson construct, however, has always been that it makes Congress, not the Constitution, the master of presidential authority. It disregards the reality that the executive is a coequal branch whose powers exist whether Congress acts or not. But the CRS prefers Jackson's conveniently airy formula, which failed to command a Court majority, to relevant opinions that don't go Congress's way, such as that of the Foreign Intelligence Court of Review—which, unlike the Supreme Court, was actually considering FISA.

Telecommunication Data

Frustrated by its inability to move public opinion, the Left is now emphasizing the large "volume of information harvested from telecommunication data and voice networks," as the *Times* breathlessly put it, "without court-approved warrants." But this is pure legerdemain [skillful deception]. When we refer to "information" from "telecommunication data," we are talking about something that, legally, is worlds apart from the content of telephone calls or e-mail messages.

These data do not include the substance of what people privately say to one another in conversations, but rather comprise statistical facts about the use of telecommunications services (for example, what phone number called another number, the date and time of the call, how long it lasted, etc.). Court warrants have never been required for the acquisition of such information because, as the Supreme Court explained over a quarter-century ago in *Smith v. Maryland*, telecommunications data do not implicate the Fourth Amendment. All phone and e-mail users know this information is conveyed to and maintained by service providers, and no one expects it to be private.

What remains real . . . is the danger to Americans implicit in any system that can't tell a war from a crime.

Analyzing such data is clearly different from monitoring the calls and e-mails themselves. For our own protection, we should want the government to collect as many of these data as possible (since doing so affects no one's legitimate privacy interests) in order to develop investigative leads. That's how a country manages to go four years without a domestic terror attack.

Yet the Left's rage continues, despite the public's evident disinterest in the mind-numbingly technical nature of the dispute, and despite the obvious truth that the NSA program was a bona fide effort to protect the nation from harm, not to snoop on Americans—only a tiny fraction of whom were affected, and those with apparent good reason. The controversy is a disquieting barometer of elite commitment to the War on Terror. As recently as two years ago, when "connecting the dots" was all the rage, liberals ignored eight years of Clintonian nonfeasance and portrayed the Bush administration as asleep at the switch while terrorists ran amok. Now they ignore President [Bill] Clinton's insistence on the very same executive surveillance power that the current administration claims and caricature Bush as the imperial president, shredding core protections of civil liberties by exaggerating the terror threat. Either way you slice it, national security becomes a game in which necessary decisions by responsible adults become political grist, and, if they get enough traction, phony scandals. What remains real, though, is the danger to Americans implicit in any system that can't tell a war from a crime.

The NSA Wiretapping Ordered by the President Was Not Unconstitutional

Wall Street Journal

The Wall Street Journal *is a major daily newspaper published in New York.*

In our current era of polarized politics, it was probably inevitable that some judge somewhere would strike down the National Security Agency's warrantless wiretaps as unconstitutional. The temptations to be hailed as Civil Libertarian of the Year are just too great.

So we suppose a kind of congratulations are due to federal Judge Anna Diggs Taylor, who won her 10 minutes of fame yesterday [August 17, 2006] for declaring that President Bush had taken upon himself "the inherent power to violate not only the laws of the Congress but the First and Fourth Amendments of the Constitution, itself." Oh, and by the way, the [President] Jimmy Carter appointee also avers that "there are no hereditary Kings in America." In case you hadn't heard.

The 44-page decision, which concludes by issuing a permanent injunction against the wiretapping program, will doubtless occasion much rejoicing among the "imperial Presidency" crowd. That may have been part of her point, as, early in the decision, Judge Taylor refers with apparent derision to "the war on terror of this Administration."

The Justice Department Will Appeal

We can at least be grateful that President Taylor's judgment won't be the last on the matter. The Justice Department immediately announced it will appeal and the injunction has been stayed for the moment. But her decision is all the more noteworthy for coming on the heels of the surveillance-driven roll up of the terrorist plot in Britain to blow up U.S.-bound airliners. In this environment, monitoring the communications of our enemies is neither a luxury nor some sinister plot to chill domestic dissent. It is a matter of life and death.

So let's set aside the judge's Star Chamber [arbitrary] rhetoric and try to examine her argument, such as it is. Take the Fourth Amendment first. The "unreasonable search and seizure" and warrant requirements of that amendment have their roots in the 18th-century abuses of the British crown. Those abuses involved the search and arrest of the King's political opponents under general and often secret warrants.

Judge Taylor sees an analogy here, but she manages to forget or overlook that no one is being denied his liberty and no evidence is being brought in criminal proceedings based on what the NSA might learn through listening to al Qaeda communications. The wiretapping program is an *intelligence* operation, not a law-enforcement proceeding. Congress was duly informed, and not a single specific domestic abuse of such a wiretap has yet been even alleged, much less found.

As for the First Amendment, Judge Taylor asserts that the plaintiffs—a group that includes the ACLU [American Civil Liberties Union] and assorted academics, lawyers and journalists who believe their conversations may have been tapped but almost surely weren't—had their free-speech rights violated because al Qaeda types are now afraid to speak to them on the phone.

But the wiretapping program is not preventing anyone from speaking on the phone. Quite the opposite—if the terrorists stopped talking on the phone, there would be nothing to wiretap. Perhaps the plaintiffs should have sued the *New York Times*, as it was that paper's disclosure of the program that created the "chill" on "free speech" that Judge Taylor laments.

The real nub of this dispute is the Constitution's idea of "inherent powers," although those two pages of her decision are mostly devoted to pouring scorn on the very concept. But jurists of far greater distinction than Judge Taylor have recognized that the Constitution vests the bulk of war-making power with the President. It did so, as the Founders explained in the *Federalist Papers*, for reasons of energy, dispatch, secrecy and accountability.

Previous Courts Ruled that the President Had Authority for Wiretaps

Before yesterday, no American court had ever ruled that the President lacked the Constitutional right to conduct such wiretaps. President Carter signed the 1978 FISA [Foreign Intelligence Surveillance Act] statute that established the special court to approve domestic wiretaps even as his Administration declared it was not ceding any Constitutional power. And in the 2002 decision *In Re: Sealed Case*, the very panel of appellate judges that hears FISA appeals noted that in a previous FISA case (*U.S. v. Truong*), a federal "court, as did all the other courts to have decided the issue, held that the President did have inherent authority to conduct warrantless searches to obtain foreign intelligence information." We couldn't find Judge Taylor's attempt to grapple with those precedents, perhaps because they'd have interfered with the lilt of her purple prose.

Unlike Judge Taylor, Presidents are accountable to the voters for their war-making decisions, as the current White House occupant has discovered. Judge Taylor can write her opinion and pose for the cameras—and no one can hold her accountable for any Americans who might die as a result.

[Editor's Note: Judge Taylor's ruling was overturned by the 6th U.S. District Court of Appeals, which held that the people who had brought suit did not have legal standing to do so.]

The President of the United States Has Broken the Law

Russ Feingold

Russ Feingold is a U.S. senator from Wisconsin.

L ast week [late January 2006] the President of the United
States gave his State of the Union address, where he spoke
of America's leadership in the world, and called on all of us to
"lead this world toward freedom." Again and again, he invoked the principle of freedom, and how it can transform nations, and empower people around the world.

But, almost in the same breath, the President openly acknowledged that he has ordered the government to spy on
Americans, on American soil, without the warrants required
by law.

The President issued a call to spread freedom throughout
the world, and then he admitted that he has deprived Americans of one of their most basic freedoms under the Fourth
Amendment—to be free from unjustified government intrusion.

*Congress has lost its way if we don't hold this President
accountable for his actions.*

The President was blunt. He said that he had authorized
the NSA's domestic spying program, and he made a number
of misleading arguments to defend himself. His words got
rousing applause from Republicans, and I think even some
Democrats.

The President was blunt, so I will be blunt: This program
is breaking the law, and this President is breaking the law. Not

Russ Feingold, statement on the Senate floor, February 7, 2006. www.commondreams
.org.

only that, he is misleading the American people in his efforts to justify this program. . . .

Congress has lost its way if we don't hold this President accountable for his actions.

Congress Understands the Threat

The President suggests that anyone who criticizes his illegal wiretapping program doesn't understand the threat we face. But we do. Every single one of us is committed to stopping the terrorists who threaten us and our families.

Defeating the terrorists should be our top national priority, and we all agree that we need to wiretap them to do it. In fact, it would be irresponsible not to wiretap terrorists. But we have yet to see any reason why we have to trample the laws of the United States to do it. The President's decision that he can break the law says far more about his attitude toward the rule of law than it does about the laws themselves.

This goes way beyond party, and way beyond politics. What the President has done here is to break faith with the American people. In the State of the Union, he also said that "we must always be clear in our principles" to get support from friends and allies that we need to fight terrorism. So let's be clear about a basic American principle: When someone breaks the law, when someone misleads the public in an attempt to justify his actions, he needs to be held accountable. The President of the United States has broken the law. The President of the United States is trying to mislead the American people. And he needs to be held accountable.

Unfortunately, the President refuses to provide any details about this domestic spying program. Not even the full Intelligence committees know the details, and they were specifically set up to review classified information and oversee the intelligence activities of our government. Instead, the President says—"Trust me.". . .

Congress Must Demand Accountability

To find out that the President of the United States has violated the basic rights of the American people is chilling. And then to see him publicly embrace his actions—and to see so many Members of Congress cheer him on—is appalling.

No one, not the President, not the Attorney General, and not any of their defenders ... has been able to explain why it is necessary to break the law to defend against terrorism.

The President has broken the law, and he has made it clear that he will continue to do so. But the President is not a king. And the Congress is not a king's court. Our job is not to stand up and cheer when the President breaks the law. Our job is to stand up and demand accountability, to stand up and check the power of an out-of-control executive branch. That is one of the reasons that the framers put us here—to ensure balance between the branches of government, not to act as a professional cheering section.

We need answers. Because no one, not the President, not the Attorney General, and not any of their defenders in this body, has been able to explain why it is necessary to break the law to defend against terrorism. And I think that's because they can't explain it.

Instead, this administration reacts to anyone who questions this illegal program by saying that those of us who demand the truth and stand up for our rights and freedoms have a pre-9/11 view of the world. In fact, the President has a pre-1776 view of the world.

Our Founders lived in dangerous times, and they risked everything for freedom. Patrick Henry said, "Give me liberty or give me death." The President's pre-1776 mentality is hurting America. It is fracturing the foundation on which our country has stood for 230 years. The President can't just bypass two branches of government, and obey only those laws he wants to obey. Deciding unilaterally which of our freedoms still apply in the fight against terrorism is unacceptable and needs to be stopped immediately.

The President's Arguments Are Baseless

Let's examine for a moment some of the President's attempts to defend his actions. His arguments have changed over time, of course. They have to—none of them hold up under even casual scrutiny, so he can't rely on one single explanation. As each argument crumbles beneath him, he moves on to a new one, until that, too, is debunked, and on and on he goes.

In the State of the Union, the President referred to Presidents in American history who cited executive authority to order warrantless surveillance. But of course those past presidents—like [Woodrow] Wilson and [Franklin] Roosevelt—were acting before the Supreme Court decided in 1967 that our communications are protected by the Fourth Amendment, and before Congress decided in 1978 that the executive branch can no longer unilaterally decide which Americans to wiretap. The Attorney General yesterday was unable to give me one example of a President who, since 1978 when FISA was passed, has authorized warrantless wiretaps outside of FISA.

So that argument is baseless, and it's deeply troubling that the President of the United States would so obviously mislead the Congress and American public. That hardly honors the Founders' idea that the President should address the Congress on the state of our union.

The Foreign Intelligence Surveillance Act [FISA] was passed in 1978 to create a secret court, made up of judges who develop national security expertise, to issue warrants for surveillance of terrorists and spies. These are the judges from whom the Bush Administration has obtained thousands of warrants since 9/11. The Administration has almost never had a warrant request rejected by those judges. They have used the FISA Court thousands of times, but at the same time they assert that FISA is an "old law" or "out of date" and they can't comply with it. Clearly they can and do comply with it— except when they don't. Then they just arbitrarily decide to go around these judges, and around the law.

No court has ever approved warrantless surveillance in violation of FISA.

The Administration has said that it ignored FISA because it takes too long to get a warrant under that law. But we know that in an emergency, where the Attorney General believes that surveillance must begin before a court order can be obtained, FISA permits the wiretap to be executed immediately as long as the government goes to the court within 72 hours. The Attorney General has complained that the emergency provision does not give him enough flexibility, he has complained that getting a FISA application together or getting the necessary approvals takes too long. But the problems he has cited are bureaucratic barriers that the executive branch put in place, and could easily remove if it wanted.

FISA also permits the Attorney General to authorize unlimited warrantless electronic surveillance in the United States during the 15 days following a declaration of war, to allow time to consider any amendments to FISA required by a wartime emergency. That is the time period that Congress specified. Yet the President thinks that he can do this indefinitely.

The Courts Have Not Approved Warrantless Wiretaps

In the State of the Union, the President also argued that federal courts had approved the use of presidential authority that he was invoking. But that turned out to be misleading as well. When I asked the Attorney General about this, he could point

me to no court—not the Supreme Court or any other court—
that has considered whether, after FISA was enacted, the President nonetheless had the authority to bypass it and authorize
warrantless wiretaps. Not one court. The Administration's effort to find support for what it has done in snippets of other
court decisions would be laughable if this issue were not so
serious.

The President knows that FISA makes it a crime to wiretap Americans in the United States without a warrant or a
court order. Why else would he have assured the public, over
and over again, that he was getting warrants before engaging
in domestic surveillance?

Here's what the President said on April 20, 2004: "Now, by
the way, any time you hear the United States government talking about wiretap, it requires—a wiretap requires a court order. Nothing has changed, by the way. When we're talking
about chasing down terrorists, we're talking about getting a
court order before we do so."

And again, on July 14, 2004: "The government can't move
on wiretaps or roving wiretaps without getting a court order.". . .

Now that the public knows about the domestic spying
program, he has had to change course. He has looked around
for arguments to cloak his actions. And all of them are completely threadbare.

The President has argued that Congress gave him authority to wiretap Americans on U.S. soil without a warrant when
it passed the Authorization for Use of Military Force after
September 11, 2001. Mr. President, that is ridiculous. Members of Congress did not think this resolution gave the President blanket authority to order these warrantless wiretaps. We
all know that. Anyone in this body who would tell you otherwise either wasn't here at the time or isn't telling the truth.
We authorized the President to use military force in Afghanistan, a necessary and justified response to September 11. We

did not authorize him to wiretap American citizens on American soil without going through the process that was set up nearly three decades ago precisely to facilitate the domestic surveillance of terrorists—with the approval of a judge. That is why both Republicans and Democrats have questioned this theory.

Congress Did Not Believe the President Could Ignore FISA

This particular claim is further undermined by congressional approval of the Patriot Act just a few weeks after we passed the Authorization for the Use of Military Force [AUMF]. The Patriot Act made it easier for law enforcement to conduct surveillance on suspected terrorists and spies, while maintaining FISA's baseline requirement of judicial approval for wiretaps of Americans in the U.S. It is ridiculous to think that Congress would have negotiated and enacted all the changes to FISA in the Patriot Act if it thought it had just authorized the President to ignore FISA in the AUMF.

In addition, in the intelligence authorization bill passed in December 2001, we extended the emergency authority in FISA, at the Administration's request, from 24 to 72 hours. Why do that if the President has the power to ignore FISA? That makes no sense at all.

None of the President's arguments explains or excuses his conduct, or the NSA's domestic spying program.

The President has also said that his inherent executive power gives him the power to approve this program. But here the President is acting in direct violation of a criminal statute. That means his power is, as Justice Jackson said in the steel seizure cases half a century ago, "at its lowest ebb." A recent letter from a group of law professors and former executive branch officials points out that "every time the Supreme Court has confronted a statute limiting the Commander-in-Chief's authority, it has upheld the statute." The Senate reports issued when FISA was enacted confirm the understanding that FISA overrode any pre-existing inherent authority of the President. As the 1978 Senate Judiciary Committee report stated, FISA "recognizes no inherent power of the president in this area." And "Congress has declared that this statute, not any claimed presidential power, controls." Contrary to what the President told the country in the State of the Union, no court has ever approved warrantless surveillance in violation of FISA.

The President's claims of inherent executive authority, and his assertions that the courts have approved this type of activity, are baseless.

The President has argued that periodic internal executive branch review provides an adequate check on the program. He has even characterized this periodic review as a safeguard for civil liberties. But we don't know what this check involves. And we do know that Congress explicitly rejected this idea of unilateral executive decision-making in this area when it passed FISA.

We cannot be a beacon of freedom for the world unless we protect our own freedoms here at home.

Finally, the president has tried to claim that informing a handful of congressional leaders, the so-called Gang of Eight, somehow excuses breaking the law. Of course, several of these members said they weren't given the full story. And all of them were prohibited from discussing what they were told. So the fact that they were informed under these extraordinary circumstances does not constitute congressional oversight, and it most certainly does not constitute congressional approval of the program. Indeed, it doesn't even comply with the National Security Act, which requires the entire memberships of the

House and Senate Intelligence Committee to be "fully and currently informed of the intelligence activities of the United States."

In addition, we now know that some of these members expressed concern about the program. The Administration ignored their protests. Just last week, one of the eight members of Congress who has been briefed about the program, Congresswoman Jane Harman, ranking member of the House Intelligence Committee, said she sees no reason why the Administration cannot accomplish its goals within the law as currently written.

The President's Conduct Cannot Be Excused

None of the President's arguments explains or excuses his conduct, or the NSA's domestic spying program. Not one. It is hard to believe that the President has the audacity to claim that they do. It is a strategy that really hinges on the credibility of the office of the Presidency itself. If you just insist that you didn't break the law, you haven't broken the law. It reminds me of what [President] Richard Nixon said after he had left office: "Well, when the president does it that means that it is not illegal." But that is not how our constitutional democracy works. Making those kinds of arguments is damaging the credibility of the Presidency.

And what's particularly disturbing is how many members of Congress have responded. They stood up and cheered. They stood up and cheered.

Justice Louis Brandeis once wrote: "Experience should teach us to be most on our guard to protect liberty when the Government's purposes are beneficent. Men born to freedom are naturally alert to repel invasion of their liberty by evil-minded rulers. The greatest dangers to liberty lurk in insidious encroachment by men of zeal, well-meaning but without understanding."

The President's actions are indefensible. Freedom is an enduring principle. It is not something to celebrate in one breath, and ignore the next. Freedom is at the heart of who we are as a nation, and as a people. We cannot be a beacon of freedom for the world unless we protect our own freedoms here at home.

The President was right about one thing. In his address, he said "We love our freedom, and we will fight to keep it."

Yes, Mr. President. We do love our freedom, and we will fight to keep it. We will fight to defeat the terrorists who threaten the safety and security of our families and loved ones. And we will fight to protect the rights of law-abiding Americans against intrusive government power.

As the President said, we must always be clear in our principles. So let us be clear: We cherish the great and noble principle of freedom, we will fight to keep it, and we will hold this President—and anyone who violates those freedoms—accountable for their actions. In a nation built on freedom, the President is not a king, and no one is above the law.

Wiretapping Without Warrants Was Not Authorized by Congress

Patrick Leahy

Patrick Leahy is a U.S. senator from Vermont.

The question for this hearing is the illegality of the Government's domestic spying on ordinary Americans without a warrant.

The question facing us is not whether the Government should have all the tools it needs to protect the American people. Of course it should. The terrorist threat to America's security remains very real, and it is vital that we be armed with the tools needed to protect Americans' security. That is why I co-authored the PATRIOT Act five years ago and why it passed with such broad, bipartisan support. That is why we have amended the Foreign Intelligence Surveillance Act five times since 9/11 to provide more flexibility.

The President and the Justice Department have a constitutional duty to faithfully execute the laws. They do not write them.

We all agree that we should be wiretapping al Qaeda terrorists—of course we should. Congress has given the President authority to monitor these messages legally, with checks to guard against abuses when Americans' conversations and email are being monitored. But instead, the President has chosen to do it illegally, without those safeguards.

A judge from the special court Congress created to monitor domestic spying would grant any request to wiretap an al Qaeda terrorist. Of the approximately 20,000 foreign intelli-

Patrick Leahy, testimony before Senate Judiciary Committee, February 6, 2006. http://leahy.senate.gov.

gence warrant applications over the past 28 years, only a handful have been turned down. . . .

The domestic spying programs into emails and telephone calls apparently conducted by the National Security Agency were first reported by the *New York Times* on December 16, 2005. The next day, President Bush admitted that secret, domestic wiretapping has been conducted without warrants since late 2001, and that he has issued secret orders in this regard more than 30 times since then. We have asked for the presidential orders, but they have not been provided. We have asked for the official legal opinions of the Government that the Administration says justify and limit this program. They, too, have been withheld from us.

This hearing is expressly about the legality of these programs, not about their operational details. In order for us to conduct effective oversight, we clearly need the official documents that answer these basic questions. We are an oversight Committee of the United States Senate—the oversight committee with jurisdiction over the Department of Justice and over its enforcement of the laws of the United States. We are the duly elected representatives of the people of the United States, and it is our duty to determine whether the laws of the United States have been violated. The President and the Justice Department have a constitutional duty to faithfully execute the laws. They do not write them. They do not pass them. They do not have unchecked power to decide what laws to follow and what laws to ignore. They cannot violate the law or the rights of ordinary Americans. In America no one, not even the President, is above the law.

The President's Domestic Spying Programs

There is much that we do not know about the President's secret spying programs. I hope that we will begin to get some real answers from the Administration today—not simply more self-serving characterizations. Let's start with what we do know.

Point One—The President's secret wiretapping program is not authorized by the Foreign Intelligence Surveillance Act (FISA).

That law expressly states that it provides the "exclusive" source of authority for wiretapping for intelligence purposes. Wiretapping that is not authorized under that statute is a federal crime. That is what the law says, and that is what the law means. This law was enacted to define how domestic surveillance for intelligence purposes may be conducted while protecting the fundamental liberties of Americans. Two or more generations of Americans are too young to know this from their experience, but there's a reason we have the FISA law. It was enacted after decades of abuses by the Executive, including the wiretapping of Dr. Martin Luther King Jr. and other political opponents of earlier government officials, and the White House "horrors" of the Nixon years, during which another President [Richard Nixon] asserted that whatever he did was legal because he was the President.

The law has been updated five times since September 11, 2001, in order to keep pace with intelligence needs and technological developments. It provides broad and flexible authority. On July 31, 2002, the Justice Department testified that this law "is a highly flexible statute that has proven effective" and noted: "When you are trying to prevent terrorist acts, that is really what FISA was intended to do and it was written with that in mind."

The Bush Administration now concedes that this President knowingly created a program involving thousands of wiretaps of Americans in the United States over the period of the last four to five years without complying with FISA. Legal scholars and former Government officials have been almost unanimous in stating the obvious: This is against the law.

Congress Did Not Authorize Illegal Wiretapping

Point Two—The Authorization for the Use of Military Force that Democratic and Republican lawmakers joined together to pass in the days immediately after the September 11 attacks did not give the President the authority to go around the FISA law to wiretap Americans illegally.

Nothing in the Authorization for the Use of Military Force was intended secretly to undermine the liberties and rights of Americans.

That resolution authorized the military action of sending military troops into Afghanistan to kill or capture Osama bin Laden and those acting with him—in the words of the statute, "to use the United States Armed Forces against those responsible for the recent attacks launched against the United States."

It did not authorize domestic surveillance of United States citizens without a warrant from a judge. Nothing in the Authorization for the Use of Military Force was intended secretly to undermine the liberties and rights of Americans. Rather, it was to defend our liberties and rights that Congress authorized the President to use our Armed Forces against those responsible for the 9/11 attacks.

Let me be clear: It is only Republican Senators who are talking about "special rights for terrorists." I have no interest in that. I wish the Bush Administration had done a better job with the vast powers Congress has given it to destroy al Qaeda and kill or capture Osama bin Laden. But it has not.

My concern is for peaceful Quakers who are being spied upon and other law-abiding Americans and babies and nuns who are placed on terrorist watch lists.

The President Never Sought Broader Legal Authority

Point Three—The President never came to Congress and never sought additional legal authority to engage in the type of domestic surveillance in which the NSA has been secretly engaged for the last several years.

After September 11, 2001, I helped lead a bipartisan effort to provide tools and legal authorities to improve our capabilities to prevent terrorist attacks. We enacted amendments to FISA in the USA PATRIOT ACT in October 2001 and four additional times subsequently. Ironically, when a Republican Senator proposed a legal change to the standard needed for a FISA warrant, the Bush Administration did not support that effort but raised questions about its constitutionality and testified that it was not needed. This Administration told the Senate that FISA was working just fine and that it did not seek additional adjustments. Attorney General Gonzales has said that the Administration did not ask for legislation authorizing warrantless wiretapping of Americans and did not think such legislation would pass.

Not only did the Bush Administration not seek broader legal authority, it kept the very existence of its domestic wiretapping program without warrants completely secret from 527 of the 535 Members of Congress, including Members on this Committee and on the Intelligence Committee, and placed limits and restrictions on what the eight Members who *were* told anything could know or say.

The Administration had not suggested to Congress and the American people that FISA was inadequate, outmoded or irrelevant until it was caught violating the statute with a secret program of wiretapping Americans without warrants. Indeed, in 2004, two years after he authorized the secret warrantless wiretapping program, the President told the American people: "Anytime you hear the United States government talking about wiretap, a wiretap requires a court order." He continued: "Nothing has changed ... When we're talking about chasing down terrorists, we're talking about getting a court order before we do so." In light of what we now know, that statement was, at best, misleading.

The Rule of Law

I have many questions for the Attorney General. But first, I have a message to give him and the President. It is a message

127

that should be unanimous, from every Member of Congress regardless of party and ideology. Under our Constitution, Congress is the co-equal branch of Government that makes the laws. If you believe we need new laws, you can come to us and tell us. If Congress agrees, we will amend the law. If you do not even attempt to persuade Congress to amend the law, you must abide by the law as written. That is as true for this President as it is for any other American. That is the rule of law, on which our Nation was founded, and on which it endures and prospers.

Arguments for the Legality of the NSA Spying Program Are Myths

David Cole

David Cole is the legal affairs correspondent at The Nation *magazine and the author of* Enemy Aliens: Double Standards and Constitutional Freedoms in the War on Terrorism *(2005).*

"When the President does it, that means that it is not illegal." So Richard Nixon infamously defended his approval of a plan to engage in warrantless wiretapping of Americans involved in the antiwar movement in the 1970s. For thirty years Nixon's defense has stood as the apogee of presidential arrogance. But of course Nixon was proved wrong. The wiretapping plan was shelved when [FBI Director] J. Edgar Hoover, of all people, objected to it. Nixon's approval of it was listed in the articles of impeachment. Nixon learned the hard way that Presidents are not above the law.

George W. Bush appears not to have learned the lesson. His defense of the National Security Agency's warrantless wiretapping of Americans resurrects the Nixon doctrine, with one modification. For Bush, "when the Commander in Chief does it, it is not illegal." In a memo to Congress, the Administration argued that the Commander in Chief may not be restricted in the "means and methods of engaging the enemy," and that Bush is thus free to wiretap Americans without court approval in the "war on terror" even if Congress has made it a crime. This assertion of uncheckable executive power is just one of five myths the Administration has propagated in a PR blitz designed to convince the public of a transparently unconvincing argument. As Congress readies for hearings on the subject, here's a primer on the spying debate.

Myth 1: Following existing law would require the NSA to turn off a wiretap of an Al Qaeda member calling in to the United States.

Variations on this theme appear every time the Administration defends the NSA spying program. The suggestion is that the Foreign Intelligence Surveillance Act (FISA) would interfere with the President's ability to monitor Al Qaeda members' calls when it's most important to do so. There's only one problem: FISA would *not* require the tap to be turned off. First, FISA does not apply at all to wiretaps targeted at foreign nationals abroad. Its restrictions are triggered only when the surveillance is targeted at a citizen or permanent resident of the United States, or when the surveillance is obtained from a wiretap physically located within the United States. If the NSA is listening in on an Al Qaeda member's phone in Pakistan, nothing in FISA requires it to stop listening if that person calls someone in the United States. Second, even when FISA is triggered, it does not require the wiretap to be turned off but merely to be approved by a judge, based on a showing of probable cause that the target is a member of a terrorist organization. Such judicial approval may be obtained after the wiretap is put in place, so long as it is approved within seventy-two hours.

The Al Qaeda authorization says not one word about wiretapping Americans.

Myth 2: Congress approved the NSA spying program when it authorized military force against Al Qaeda.

This argument cannot be squared with existing law, which provides that even when Congress declares war—a much more formal and grave step than an authorization to use force—the President has only fifteen days to conduct warrantless surveillance. The Al Qaeda authorization says not one word about wiretapping Americans. In addition, when asked why the Administration did not seek to amend FISA to permit this program, the Attorney General explained that he consulted with several members of Congress but that they told him it would be "difficult, if not impossible," to obtain permission. You can't argue that you didn't ask because Congress would have said no, but that without asking, and without Congress saying so, it actually said yes.

The fact that Presidents may have "inherent" authority to take action . . . does not mean they have uncheckable authority to do so once Congress has prohibited the conduct.

Myth 3: Bush informed Congress of the NSA program.

"If I wanted to break the law, why was I briefing Congress?" Bush asked in a speech on the spying issue. His Administration claims that it informed isolated members of Congress twelve times, but there is no evidence that it told those members either that it believed its actions were authorized by the use-of-force resolution or that it was asserting executive power to violate criminal law. In addition, the briefings were classified, and members were prohibited from repeating to other members anything that was said there. So the answer to Bush's question is that he may have "informed Congress" precisely to provide cover in case his secret lawbreaking ever became public, but he did so in a manner that insured Congress could not take action against him.

Myth 4: The courts have upheld inherent presidential power to conduct warrantless wiretapping for foreign intelligence purposes.

Bush's defenders claim that every court to address the subject has said the President has inherent authority to conduct war rantless wiretapping for foreign intelligence-gathering purposes. What they do not say is that those courts were addressing presidential authority *before* Congress regulated such activity by enacting FISA in 1978. The fact that Presidents may have "inherent" authority to take action in the absence of contrary Congressional intent does not mean they have uncheckable authority to do so once Congress has prohibited the conduct. That argument would mean FISA is unconstitutional, and no court has so ruled.

Myth 5: The President as Commander in Chief cannot be regulated by Congress.

The Administration's ultimate defense is that even if Bush broke the law, his constitutional authority as Commander in Chief permits him to do so at his discretion. According to the Justice Department, Congress cannot limit his choice of how to "engage the enemy." This rationale is not limited to wiretapping. On the same theory, Justice argued in 2002 that he could order torture despite a criminal statute to the contrary. It is that theory that Bush was presumably invoking when, in signing the amendment barring "cruel, inhuman and degrading treatment" of terrorism suspects, he said he would interpret it "in a manner consistent with the constitutional authority of the President to supervise the unitary executive branch and as Commander in Chief."

Bush tried this theory out on the Supreme Court in the Guantánamo cases, when he argued that it would be an unconstitutional intrusion on his Commander in Chief powers to extend habeas corpus review to Guantánamo detainees. Not a single Justice on the Court accepted that radical proposition. But that hasn't stopped Bush from asserting it again. After all, when you get to say what the law is, what's a contrary Supreme Court precedent or two?

Illegal NSA Spying Takes Resources Away from Critical Investigations

Ira Winkler

Ira Winkler is president of the Internet Security Advisors Group. He is a former National Security Agency analyst and the author of the book Spies Among Us.

As a former NSA analyst, I'm dismayed by the continuing revelations of the National Security Agency's warrant-less—and therefore illegal—spying. The case involves fundamental issues related to NSA's missions and long-standing rules of engagement. What's even more dismaying is the lack of public reaction to this.

Fundamentally, this is an issue of law. FISA, the Foreign Intelligence Surveillance Act, was established in 1978 to address a wide variety of issues revolving around Watergate, during which a president used foreign intelligence agencies to collect data on U.S. citizens. As part of FISA, the NSA has to get warrants to analyze and maintain collections of data involving U.S. citizens. FISA has withstood all tests until now, and it involves a fundamental aspect of the U.S. Constitution—its system of checks and balances.

The FISA law allows NSA to request those warrants up to 72 hours after the fact—that is, after the data has been analyzed. And lest you think that the courts from which such warrants are requested are staffed by a bunch of liberal, activist, criminal-coddling judges, they have reportedly turned down only five warrants in the last 28 years. So when President Bush says, "If Osama bin Laden is calling someone in the United States, we want to know about it," followed by his ner-

Ira Winkler, "Why NSA Spying Puts the U.S. in Danger," *Computerworld*, May 16, 2006. www.computerworld.com. Reproduced by permission.

vous laugh, he's laughing at the American public, since "knowing about it" is a totally irrelevant issue. FISA blocks no legitimate acquistion of knowledge.

It doesn't even slow the process down. The issue is not that the NSA cannot examine calls into the U.S. from terrorist suspects—FISA provides for that—but that the agency must justify acting on the results and keeping the information within 72 hours. The president claims that the process of getting those warrants—of complying with the law—is too time-consuming. Normally, that would sound like simple laziness, but the reality is that the program is so large that they would need an army of lawyers to get all the warrants they'd need to be in compliance with FISA. But the law is the law. No president has the right to pick and choose which laws they find convenient to follow.

We have snakes in our midst, yet we are chasing a mythical beast with completely unreliable evidence.

If Bush didn't like the FISA laws, he could have asked Congress to amend them. After all, after 9/11 Congress passed a wide variety of laws (without, for the most part, reading them) that were supposed to prevent another attack. They could have easily slipped something modifying FISA into all of that legislation. They did not, though recent revelations about this administration's use of signing statements may indicate that they simply didn't want to raise the possibility of questions.

Wasted Effort and Loss of Credibility

Ignoring FISA's rules concerning warrants is illegal. It also weakens national security, since the process of obtaining the warrants has an effect on quality control. To date, FBI agents have been sent out to do thousands of investigations based on this warrantless wiretapping. None of those investigations turned up a legitimate lead. I have spoken to about a dozen agents, and they all roll their eyes and indicate disgust with the man-years of wasted effort being put into physically examining NSA "leads."

This scattershot attempt at data mining drags FBI agents away from real investigations, while destroying the NSA's credibility in the eyes of law enforcement and the public in general. That loss of credibility makes the NSA the agency that cried wolf—and after so many false leads, should they provide something useful, the data will be looked at skeptically and perhaps given lower priority by law enforcement than it would otherwise have been given.

Worse, FBI agents working real and pressing investigations such as organized crime, child pornography and missing persons are being pulled away from their normal law enforcement duties to follow up on NSA leads. Nobody wants another 9/11, of course, but we experience real crimes on a daily basis that, over the course of even one year, cause far greater loss of life and damage than the 9/11 attacks did. There are children abused on a daily basis to facilitate online child pornography, yet I know of at least two agents who were pulled from their duties tracking down child abusers to investigate everyone who called the same pizza parlor as a person who received a call from a person who received an overseas call. There are plenty of similar examples.

The courts and Congress do not appear to have a clue as to the full extent of the program.

We have snakes in our midst, yet we are chasing a mythical beast with completely unreliable evidence.

And now we discover that the NSA is searching through every possible phone call made in the U.S. They claim that the NSA is not receiving any personally identifying information. Frankly, you have to be a complete moron to believe that. It is trivial to narrow down access to a phone number to just a few members of a household, if not in fact to exactly one person.

The government claims that it got the information legally since it was given the data or bought it from the telecom companies. Perhaps, but *USA Today* reports that at least one company (Qwest) received threats from the U.S government for not cooperating. That's extortion—another crime.

Congress is not exercising any backbone at all, and neither are its constituents—a.k.a, you. Every time we receive new information about the NSA domestic spying program, it gets exponentially worse, and it's clear that we still have no clue as to the full extent of the program. More importantly, the courts and Congress do not appear to have a clue as to the full extent of the program, and those bodies are constitutionally required to exercise checks and balances over the NSA. The actions taken by the executive branch after 9/11 aren't protecting our freedom. They are usurping it.

Invasion of Privacy

So, besides knowing that it's illegal, that is provides useless information, that it takes law enforcement agents away from investigating and preventing crimes actually being committed, and that it erodes civil liberties, we have no clue how bad it really is. The arguments I hear for it are that 1) I have nothing to worry about so I don't care if they investigate me, 2) we need to do everything we can to protect ourselves, or 3) the NSA isn't listening to the content of the calls, so there's no harm.

We have ... pulled law enforcement agents away from real ongoing crimes to investigate poor and scattered "intelligence."

Addressing the first point, people who did nothing wrong have been investigated and jailed in this country and others over the years. Additionally, I believe that Saddam Hussein would cheerfully agree with the tired allegation that if you did nothing wrong, you shouldn't mind the government looking at your calls. I think Lenin, Stalin, Hitler and the Chinese government would also agree with that line of thought. Is this the company we consent to keep in the name of safety?

To doing everything we can to protect ourselves, we have, again, pulled law enforcement agents away from real ongoing crimes to investigate poor and scattered "intelligence." This definition of "protection," again, leaves us watching for dragons while very real snakes multiply freely in our midst.

And so what if the NSA isn't listening to the calls themselves? An intelligence agency doesn't need to hear your chatter to invade your privacy. By simply tying numbers together—an intelligence discipline of traffic analysis—I assure you I can put together a portrait of your life. I'll know your friends, your hobbies, where your children go to school, if you're having an affair, whether you plan to take a trip and even when you're awake or asleep. Give me a list of whom you're calling and I can tell most of the critical things I need to know about you.

The domestic spying program has gotten so massive that the well-established process of getting a warrant cannot be followed—and quantity most certainly doesn't translate to quality.

Unnerved at the prospect of one person holding that data? You should be. While I can personally attest to the fact that the vast majority of NSA employees are good and honest people, the NSA has more than its share of bitter, vindictive mid- and senior-level bureaucrats. I would not trust my personal information with these people, since I have personally seen them use internal information against their enemies.

At the same time, we have seen the Bush administration go after Joesph Wilson, the ambassador who spoke out against the Bush administration, by leaking potentially classified information about him. They vigorously tried to undermine the credibility of Richard Clarke and others who spoke out against them. Now consider that the NSA telephone call database is not classified; there's no legal reason that they can't use this database as vindictively as they did, even when the data was potentially classified, as in releasing the information that Valerie Plame, Wilson's wife, worked for the CIA.

Over the years, I have defended the NSA and its employees as reasonable and law abiding. I was all for invading Afghanistan, deployment of the Clipper Chip and many other controversial government programs. NSA domestic spying is against everything I was ever taught working at the NSA. I might be more for it if there was any credible evidence that this somehow provides useful information that couldn't otherwise be had. However, the domestic spying program has gotten so massive that the well-established process of getting a warrant cannot be followed—and quantity most certainly doesn't translate to quality. Quite the opposite.

Again, I'm not arguing against allowing the NSA or other intelligence agencies to collect information on terrorists. My problem is that they are bypassing legally required oversight mechanisms. This implies that the operations are massive, and go well beyond the scope of looking at terrorists. Not only is this diminishing what makes America unique and worth preserving, it removes all quality control and puts the country at increased risks by moving resources away from critical investigations of more substantial threats.

I think Sen. Jon Ky, a strong supporter of the NSA domestic spying program, said it best: "We have got to collect intelligence on the enemy." I fully agree. But the enemy numbers in the hundreds at best. The NSA is collecting data on hundreds of millions of people who are clearly not the enemy. These numbers speak for themselves.

CHAPTER 3

Should the Foreign Intelligence Surveillance Act (FISA) Be Modernized?

Overview: Congress Is Debating Whether to Make Permanent Changes to the FISA

Tom A. Peter

Tom A. Peter is a staff writer for the Christian Science Monitor, *a daily international newspaper.*

Politicians are once again debating the legality of the controversial "Protect America Act," which amended the Foreign Intelligence Surveillance Act (FISA) to allow for warrantless wiretapping. The law's Feb. 1, 2008 expiration date is approaching. President George Bush and his supporters are pushing to make the law permanent. Meanwhile, opponents are raising familiar concerns about the protection of civil liberties. On Thursday [September 20, 2007] J. Michael McConnell, director of national intelligence, testified before Congress that not only was the law a necessity, but that public debate about it will cost American lives by exposing American surveillance methods to the nation's enemies. Opponents in Congress were critical of Mr. McConnell's remarks.

On Wednesday [September 19, 2007], Bush visited the National Security Agency and called for support to make the Protect America Act a permanent law, reports the *E-Commerce Times*. The temporary act was rushed into law last month [August 2007] and allows US intelligence agencies to monitor phone conversations between US citizens calling suspected terrorists overseas.

> "The threat from Al-Qaeda is not going to expire in 135 days," Bush warned during a Wednesday visit to the National Security Agency (NSA) in Fort Meade, Md. "Unless

Tom A. Peter, "Bush Wants Permanent Warrantless Wiretap Law," *Christian Science Monitor*, September 22, 2007. Reproduced by permission from *Christian Science Monitor*, www.csmonitor.com.

the FISA reforms in the act are made permanent, our national security professionals will lose critical tools they need to protect our country," he said. "Without these tools, it'll be harder to figure out what our enemies are doing to train, recruit and infiltrate operatives in our country. Without these tools our country will be much more vulnerable to attack."

During his testimony to Congress McConnell told representatives that "intelligence business is conducted in secret," and that public examination of these laws had compromised their effectiveness by exposing their inner-workings, reports the *Los Angeles Times*.

> "It's conducted in secret for a reason," McConnell told the House Intelligence Committee. "You compromise sources and methods, and what this debate has allowed those who wish us harm to do is to understand significantly more about how we were targeting their communications."

> Asked by Rep. Anna G. Eshoo (D-Calif.) if he thought that congressional questioning of the administration's intelligence program would lead to the killing of Americans, McConnell said, "Yes, ma'am, I do." Eshoo called his assessment "a stretch."

Democrats also expressed that they want to give the administration the necessary tools to monitor foreign targets, they also want to ensure that checks and balances are maintained, reports the *Congressional Quarterly*. They also expressed particular concern about the portion of the law that allows for electronic surveillance of foreign terror suspects that results in warrantless wiretapping of US citizens within the country.

> Panel Republicans and McConnell then tried to turn the tables on Democrats. They highlighted a case where they said spying restrictions in place prior to passage of the temporary six-month legislation had delayed for 12 hours an attempt to rescue U.S. soldiers captured by insurgents in Iraq.

> The tense hearing demonstrated the frayed relations between congressional Democrats and McConnell going into

the high-stakes negotiations about permanent changes to the Foreign Intelligence Surveillance Act. . . .

In a press release, the American Civil Liberties Union (ACLU) contended that many of the reasons being used to justify the need for the warrantless wiretapping law are mere myths. The ACLU attacked two key justifications, among others, for warrantless wiretapping: that Americans will not be affected by the law and that FISA needed to be expanded because of new technologies. The ACLU also challenged McConnell's contention that without the law, bureaucracy made the wiretapping process ineffectually slow.

> Myth: McConnell said that it takes 200 "man" hours to get a court order to access a telephone number.

> Reality: The math, courtesy of Wired.com. "In 2006, the government filed 2,181 such applications with the Foreign Intelligence Surveillance court. The court approved 2,176 2006 FISA Warrant Applications. That means government employees spent 436,200 hours writing out foreign intelligence wiretaps in 2006. That's 53,275 workdays." The numbers have been greatly exaggerated. . . .

> Even if it is merely a resource issue, there were and are bipartisan bills that would streamline the application process and grant more resources. Besides, there is no "too-much-paperwork" exception to the Fourth Amendment.

Under the new law, private telecommunications firms that worked with the government to enable wiretapping and other surveillance methods are freed from any legal liability, reports *CNET*. Bush hopes to make this law a retroactive policy.

> "It's particularly important for Congress to provide meaningful liability protection to those companies now facing multibillion-dollar lawsuits only because they are believed to have assisted in efforts to defend our nation, following the 9/11 attacks," Bush said.

The Electronic Frontier Foundation, which has sued AT&T over its allegedly illegal cooperation with the government, says references to the crippling liability posed by such suits suggest that the scope of the wiretapping is "massive."

"The statutory penalties for warrantless wiretapping are relatively small per person—even if AT&T was ordered to pay the maximum penalty, a few hundred illegal wiretaps would amount to less than a rounding error in the phone company's quarterly statements," EFF attorney Kurt Opsahl wrote in a recent blog entry. "If the NSA was truly limiting its spying to suspected terrorists, the potential liability would be like an annoying gnat on an elephant. So why are the companies so worried?"

[EDITOR'S NOTE: The viewpoints that follow are from the Congressional debate that preceded passage of the Protect America Act, which made temporary changes to the FISA.]

The Best Way to End the Debate about NSA Wiretapping Is to Amend the FISA

Richard A. Posner

Richard A. Posner is a judge of the U.S. Court of Appeals for the Seventh Circuit and a senior lecturer at the University of Chicago Law School.

The best, and probably the only, way to end the debate over the propriety of the National Security Agency's conducting electronic surveillance outside the framework of the Foreign Intelligence Surveillance Act is for Congress to amend the Act to create a legal regime that will enable such surveillance to be conducted without infringing civil liberties or invading privacy—but also without compromising national security.

FISA, enacted in 1978—long before the danger of global terrorism was recognized and electronic surveillance was transformed by the digital revolution—is dangerously obsolete. It retains value as a framework for monitoring the communications of known terrorists, but it is hopeless as a framework for detecting terrorists. It requires that surveillance be conducted pursuant to warrants based on probable cause to believe that the target of surveillance *is* a terrorist, when the desperate need is to find out *who* is a terrorist. In the words of General Michael Hayden, director of NSA on 9/11 and now director of the CIA, the NSA program is designed to "detect and prevent," whereas "FISA was built for long-term coverage against known agents of an enemy power." Yet in combating terrorism "the problem of defeating the enemy consists very largely of finding him."

Richard A. Posner, "How to Make Warrantless Electronic Surveillance Accountable without Endangering National Security," testimony prepared for a hearing before the U.S. House Permanent Select Committee on Intelligence, July 19, 2006.

Searching for Clues

Critics of NSA's program point out that surveillance not cabined by a probable-cause requirement produces many false positives (intercepts that prove upon investigation to have no intelligence value). That is not a sound criticism. National security intelligence is a search for a needle in a haystack. The intelligence services must cast a wide net with a fine mesh to catch the clues that may enable the next terrorist attack on the United States to be prevented. The initial trolling for clues is done by computer search programs, which do not invade privacy because search programs are not sentient beings. The programs pick out a tiny percentage of communications to be read by (human) intelligence officers, and a subset of these communications will turn out to have intelligence value and spur an investigation. Some of these may be communications to which a U.S. citizen or permanent resident is a party.

The NSA is also believed to have obtained millions of phone records from telephone companies to enable the agency to engage in "traffic analysis." That means analyzing the phone traffic (the outside of the envelope, as it were) rather than the contents of the phone conversations (the inside of the envelope). Suppose the NSA has the phone number of a known or suspected terrorist. It can use its database of phone numbers to determine the most frequent numbers called to or from that number and then determine the most frequent numbers called to or from *those* numbers and in this way trace a possible terrorist network—all without listening to any conversation. That comes later.

The government can't get a warrant just to find out whether someone is a terrorist; it has to already have a reason to believe that he is one.

Such programs are vital, given the terrorist menace, which is real—and, as recent terrorist activities in places as far apart as Canada, Israel, and India suggest, are growing. This city, the capital of the United States, could be destroyed by an atomic bomb the size of a melon, which if coated with lead would be undetectable. The city could be rendered uninhabitable, perhaps for decades, merely by the explosion of a conventional bomb that had been coated with radioactive material. Smallpox virus bioengineered to make the virus even more toxic and the vaccine ineffectual, then aerosolized and sprayed in a major airport, could kill millions of people. Our terrorist enemies have the will to do such things and abundant opportunities, because our borders are porous both to enemies and to containers. They will soon have the means as well. Access to weapons of mass destruction is becoming ever easier, especially access to biological weaponry, which is simple and cheap to make and easy to conceal and disseminate.

The Problem with Warrants

Most likely the next terrorist attack on the United States, like the 9/11 attacks, will be mounted from inside the country but be orchestrated by leaders safely ensconced somewhere abroad. So suppose the NSA learns the phone number of a suspected terrorist in a foreign country. If the agency wants just to listen in to his calls to other people abroad, FISA doesn't require a warrant. But it does if either (1) one party to the call is in the United States and the interception takes place here or (2) the party on the U.S. side of the conversation is a "U.S person"— primarily either a citizen or a permanent resident. If both parties are in the United States, no warrant *can* be issued; interception is prohibited. But as a practical matter the government cannot get a warrant in the "U.S. person" situation either, in the case that I have posited, because the statute requires grounds for believing that such a person is a foreign spy or a terrorist. Even if a person is here just on a student or tourist visa, or on no visa, the government can get a warrant only if it has probable cause to believe him an agent of a foreign power or a terrorist group. In either case, the government can't get a warrant just to find out whether someone is a terrorist; it has to already have a reason to believe that he is one.

It may be thanks to programs such as the NSA's non-FISA surveillance, as well as to other counterterrorist operations, that we have been spared a repetition of 9/11. We must not let our guard down, basking in the false assurance created by the lapse of time since the last attack. The legality of the NSA program has been called into question, and fears have been expressed about its impact on civil liberties and on privacy. Fortunately, Congress can allay these concerns without gutting the program. But not by amending FISA to relax the standard for obtaining a warrant. Instead of requiring probable cause to believe the target a terrorist, FISA could, no doubt, be amended to require merely reasonable suspicion. But even that would be too restrictive. It is not enough to be able to monitor suspects; they must be found. Moreover, the lower the standard for getting a warrant, the more porous the filter that a requirement of a warrant creates. If all that the government is required to state in its application for a warrant is that it thinks an interception might yield intelligence information, judges will have no basis for refusing to grant the application. The requirement of a warrant will be a figleaf.

Warrants are neither the best nor the only method of allaying the concerns that comprehensive electronic surveillance for purposes of national-security intelligence engenders.

The preoccupation of civil libertarians with warrants is anachronistic. The government's easy access to the vast databases compiled by private and public entities for purposes unrelated to national security has enabled it to circumvent the privacy interests that civil libertarians look to warrant requirements to protect. Fortunately, other modes of protecting civil liberties and privacy are available.

Proposed Amendments

Concretely, I suggest that Congress amend FISA to authorize warrantless electronic surveillance to obtain national-security intelligence but at the same time subject that surveillance to tight oversight and specific legal controls, as follows:

1. *Oversight*: The amendment would—

a. Create a steering committee for national security electronic surveillance composed of the Attorney General, the Director of National Intelligence, the Secretary of Homeland Security (chairman), and a senior or retired federal judge or Justice appointed by the Chief Justice of the United States. The committee would monitor all such surveillance to assure compliance with the Constitution and laws.

b. Require the NSA to submit to the FISA court, every six months, a list of the names and other identifying information of all persons whose communications had been intercepted without a warrant in the preceding six months, with a brief statement of why these individuals had been targeted. If the court concluded that an interception had been inappropriate, it would so report to the steering committee and the congressional intelligence oversight committees. Alternatively, the list could be required to be submitted directly to the oversight committees. In addition, judicial officers employed by the FISA court could be stationed in the NSA to monitor its data-mining activities for compliance with law.

2. *Specific controls*: The amendment would—

a. Authorize "national security electronic surveillance" outside FISA's existing framework, provided that the President certified that such surveillance was necessary and proper in the national interest. Warrants would continue to be required for all physical searches and for all electronic surveillance for which FISA's existing probable-cause requirement could be satisfied.

b. Define "national security" narrowly, excluding "ecoterrorism," animal-rights terrorism, and other forms of political violence that, though criminal and deplorable, do not endanger the nation.

c. Sunset after five years, or sooner if the declaration of national emergency was rescinded.

d. Forbid *any* use of intercepted information for any purpose other than "national security" as narrowly defined in the amendment (point b above). Thus the information could not be used as evidence or leads in a prosecution for ordinary crime. Violations of this provision would be made felonies punishable by long prison sentences and heavy fines, to allay concern that "wild talk" picked up by electronic surveillance would lead to criminal investigations unrelated to national security. No one wants strangers eavesdropping on his personal conversations. But the principal reason for this aversion is fear of what the strangers might do with the information to harm one, and that fear can be allayed by forbidding the use of information obtained by surveillance conducted to detect terrorist activity for any purpose other than to protect national security. So if the NSA discovered that an American was not a terrorist but was evading income tax, it could not refer its discovery to the Justice Department or the Internal Revenue Service to enable the person to be prosecuted for tax evasion or sued for back taxes.

e. Require responsible officials to certify to the FISA court annually that there had been no violations of the statute during the preceding year. False certification would be punishable as perjury.

f. Bar lawsuits challenging the legality of the NSA's current warrantless surveillance program. Such lawsuits would distract officials from their important duties, to no purpose given the amendment.

The point to be particularly emphasized is that warrants are neither the best nor the only method of allaying the concerns that comprehensive electronic surveillance for purposes of national-security intelligence engenders. By amending FISA to place such surveillance under high-level supervision, restrict (under pain of heavy criminal penalties) the uses that can be made of information obtained by the surveillance, assure judicial and congressional access to the records of the surveillance, and establish the other controls that I have suggested, Congress can protect civil liberties and privacy without undermining national security.

The FISA Is Not Compatible with Technological Change

Kenneth L. Wainstein

As of 2008 Kenneth L. Wainstein was the assistant attorney general of the U.S. Department of Justice National Security Division.

In order to explain why we must modernize FISA [the Foreign Intelligence Surveillance Act of 1978] today, it is important to understand what Congress intended to accomplish when it drafted FISA almost thirty years ago. I will therefore begin my testimony today with a brief discussion of the context in which FISA was enacted. Then I will explain how sweeping changes since 1978—both in the nature of the threat that we face and in telecommunications technologies—have upset the delicate balance that Congress sought to achieve when it enacted FISA. As a result of these changes, FISA now regulates many intelligence activities of the sort that Congress sought to exclude from the scope of FISA—an unintended consequence that has impaired our intelligence capabilities. . . .

The Scope of FISA in 1978

Congress enacted FISA in 1978 for the purpose of establishing a "statutory procedure authorizing the use of electronic surveillance in the United States for foreign intelligence purposes." The legislation came on the heels of the Church Committee Report, which disclosed abuses of domestic national security surveillances, and reflected a judgment that the civil liberties of Americans would be well-served by the development of a process for court approval of foreign intelligence surveillance activities directed at individuals in the United States. To accomplish this objective, Congress authorized the

Kenneth L. Wainstein, testimony before the Select Committee on Intelligence, U.S. Senate, May 1, 2007.

Attorney General to make an application to a newly established court—the Foreign Intelligence Surveillance Court (or "FISA Court")—seeking a court order approving the use of "electronic surveillance" against foreign powers or their agents.

However, in making these changes, Congress recognized the importance of striking an appropriate balance between the need to protect the civil liberties of Americans, and the imperative that the Government be able to collect effectively foreign intelligence information that is vital to the national security. It also recognized that the terrain in which it was legislating touched upon a core Executive Branch function—the Executive's constitutional responsibility to protect the United States from foreign threats. Congress attempted to accommodate these potentially competing concerns by applying FISA's process of judicial approval to certain intelligence activities (almost all of which occur within the United States), while excluding from FISA's regime of court supervision the vast majority of overseas foreign intelligence surveillance activities, including most surveillance focused on foreign targets. The intent of Congress generally to exclude these intelligence activities from FISA's reach is expressed clearly in the House Permanent Select Committee on Intelligence's report, which explained: "[t]he committee has explored the feasibility of broadening this legislation to apply overseas, but has concluded that certain problems and unique characteristics involved in overseas surveillance preclude the simple extension of this bill to overseas surveillances."

Congress could not have foreseen international terrorism on a scale that amounts to armed conflict.

The mechanism by which Congress gave effect to this intent was its careful definition of "electronic surveillance," the term that identifies which government activities fall within FISA's scope. This statutory definition is complicated and difficult to parse, in part because it defines "electronic surveillance" by reference to particular communications technologies that were in place in 1978. (Indeed, as will be explained shortly, it is precisely FISA's use of technology-dependent provisions that has caused FISA to apply to activities today that we submit its drafters never intended.) The fact that many of the intelligence activities at issue are highly classified further complicates any effort to explain these provisions in an unclassified setting.

What Congress Intended

By reading the plain text of these provisions in light of the telecommunications communications technologies available at the time of FISA's passage, however, we can learn a great deal both about what Congress intended to cover and about what intelligence activities it intended to exclude from FISA. Consider at the outset the first definition of electronic surveillance, which encompasses the acquisition of "the contents of any wire or radio communication sent by or intended to be received by *a particular, known United States person who is in the United States,* if the contents are acquired by intentionally targeting that United States person, under circumstances in which a person has a reasonable expectation of privacy and a warrant would be required for law enforcement purposes." In other words, if the Government intentionally targets a particular, known U.S. person in the United States for foreign intelligence purposes, it is within FISA's scope, period.

A close reading of FISA's definition of "electronic surveillance" in context makes a related point clear: if the Government directed surveillance at the communications of a person overseas, those acquisitions were generally excluded from FISA's scope. The key here is the third definition of electronic surveillance, which encompasses the acquisition of "radio communications" if "both the sender and all intended recipients are in the United States." In 1978, almost all transoceanic communications into and out of the United States were radio communications carried by satellite. Accordingly, when FISA was enacted, the acquisition of most international communications would become "electronic surveillance" only if either (i) the acquisition intentionally targeted a U.S. person in the United States (in which case the acquisition would have fallen within the scope of the first definition, discussed above); or (ii) *all* of the participants to the communication were located in the United States (in which case the acquisition would fall within the third definition). Therefore, in 1978, if the government acquired communications by targeting a foreign person overseas, it usually was not engaged in "electronic surveillance"—a result consistent with Congress's expressed intent, discussed above, to carve out most overseas intelligence activities.

When FISA was enacted, almost all local calls were carried on a wire and almost all transoceanic communications were radio communications. Today that situation is almost precisely reversed.

It is important to note, however, that Congress created this carve-out by using the manner in which communications are transmitted as a proxy for the types of targets and communications that the statute intended to reach. As discussed below, this technology-dependent approach has had dramatic unintended consequences and has resulted in sweeping into FISA a wide range of intelligence activities that Congress intended to exclude from FISA in 1978. And FISA's use of technology-dependent language is not limited to these core definitions of "electronic surveillance." The distinction between "wire" and "radio" communications runs throughout the statute, and the statute also contains a provision authorizing the acquisition of communications "transmitted by means of communications used exclusively between or among foreign powers" that was premised upon the telecommunications technologies of the 1970s.

In addition to reflecting the technology of the time, the Act's legislative history also shows that the world was a different place when FISA was enacted. In terms of civil liberties, one of Congress's primary concerns was preventing the improper collection and dissemination of information about Americans involved in the civil rights movement and political activities. In terms of threats, Congress was, in large part, concerned with espionage by agents of the Soviet Union. The United States had not yet confronted the perils of large-scale international terrorism within the homeland, and the faces of terrorism were groups such as Black September, the Baader-Meinhof Group, and the Japanese Red Army. It was a time when Congress was worried that, if a terrorist hijacked an airplane, the purpose would be "to force the government to release a certain class of prisoners or to suspend aid to a particular country" not murder 3,000 innocent men, women, and children. Congress could not have foreseen international terrorism on a scale that amounts to armed conflict.

The Unintended Consequences of Technological Change

As this Committee is aware, there have been revolutions in telecommunications technology since 1978. For example, when FISA was enacted, almost all local calls were carried on a wire and almost all transoceanic communications were radio communications. Today that situation is almost precisely reversed, as most long-haul communications are on a wire and local calls often travel by air. And of course, today we have wholly new methods of communicating—such as cell phones and e-mail—that either did not exist or were not in popular use in 1978. The drafters of the FISA did not and could not have anticipated these developments.

These unanticipated advances in technology have wreaked havoc on the delicate balance that Congress originally struck when it enacted FISA. Most importantly, those advances have largely upended FISA's intended carve-out of intelligence activities directed at persons overseas. As a result, the scope of FISA has been expanded radically, without any conscious choice by the Congress, to encompass a wide range of activities that FISA did not cover in 1978.

While a thorough description of these consequences can be discussed only in a classified session, I can state the bottom line here: considerable resources of the Executive Branch and the FISA Court are now expended on obtaining court orders to monitor the communications of terrorist suspects overseas. I believe most Americans would be surprised and dismayed to discover that America's intelligence agencies routinely use scarce resources to make a showing of probable cause, a notion derived from the Fourth Amendment, and obtain a court order before acquiring the communications of these individuals. To make matters worse, these individuals frequently are communicating with other persons outside the United States. In certain cases, this process of obtaining a court order slows, and in some cases may prevent, the Government's efforts to conduct surveillance of communications that are potentially vital to the national security.

This unintended expansion of FISA's scope has hampered our intelligence capabilities and has caused us to expend resources on obtaining court approval to conduct intelligence activities directed at foreign persons overseas. This expansion of FISA's reach has necessarily diverted resources that would be better spent on protecting the privacy interests of United States persons here in the United States.

What Congress Should Do

We can and should amend FISA to restore its original focus on foreign intelligence activities that substantially implicate the privacy interests of individuals in the United States. The best way to restore that focus (and to reinstate the original carve-out for surveillance directed at foreign persons overseas) is to redefine the term "electronic surveillance" in a technology-neutral manner. Rather than focusing, as FISA does today, on *how* a communication travels or *where it* is intercepted, we should define FISA's scope by reference to *who is the subject of the surveillance.* If the surveillance is directed at a person in the United States, FISA generally should apply; if the surveillance is directed at persons overseas, it shouldn't. This would provide the Intelligence Community with much needed speed and agility while, at the same time, refocusing FISA's privacy protections on United States persons located in the United States. . . .

Rather than focusing, as FISA does today, on how *a communication travels or* where *it is intercepted, we should define FISA's scope by reference to* who is the subject of the surveillance.

In addition to this critical change in the definition of "electronic surveillance," the Administration's proposal—which draws from a number of thoughtful bills introduced in Congress during its last session—also would make several other salutary changes to FISA. . . . I will briefly summarize a few of the core changes here. First, it would amend the statutory definition of "agent of a foreign power"—a category of individuals the government may target under FISA—to include any person other than a U.S. person who possesses or is expected to transmit or receive foreign intelligence information within the United States. Second, the bill would fill a gap in our laws by permitting the Government to direct communications companies to assist in the conduct of lawful communications intelligence activities that do not constitute "electronic surveillance" under FISA, and ensuring that they are protected from liability for having assisted the government in its counterterrorism efforts. Third, the bill would streamline the FISA application process in a manner that will make FISA more efficient, while at the same time ensuring that the FISA Court has the essential information it needs to evaluate a FISA application. The other sections of the proposal, ... work in concert with these provisions to ensure our security while preserving the civil liberties of Americans. ...

I would like to address one other theme that has arisen regarding FISA modernization. Some have suggested that amending FISA is unnecessary, either because Congress has modified FISA several times since September 11th, or because they believe that increased resources could address any problems with the statute. Congress has acted wisely in making several changes to FISA that were necessary and which improved the security of our nation. However, to address our shared goal of detecting and preventing another terrorist attack, we submit that it also is necessary to update the framework governing foreign intelligence surveillance to reflect today's very different telecommunications technologies and threats. Likewise, although additional resources are always welcome, committing even substantial additional funds and other resources would not solve all of the problems posed by the current FISA framework. We should restore FISA to its original focus on establishing a framework for judicial approval of the interception of communications that substantially implicate the privacy interests of individuals in the United States; changes at the margins will not enable us to achieve this goal. ...

Restore FISA's Original Focus

For reasons that could not have been anticipated by Congress in 1978, FISA no longer reflects the delicate balance that Congress intended to strike when it enacted the statute. Radical technological changes in telecommunications have resulted in a vast array of overseas intelligence activities that were originally excluded from FISA being swept within FISA's scope. The proposal that the Administration has submitted to the Congress would restore FISA to its original focus on the protection of the privacy interests of Americans—a change that would both improve our intelligence capabilities and ensure that scarce Executive Branch and judicial resources are devoted to the oversight of intelligence activities that most clearly implicate the privacy interests of Americans. We look forward to working with the Congress to achieve these critical goals.

The FISA Is Not Adequate to Meet the Current Threat

K. A. Taipale

K. A. Taipale is executive director of the Center for Advanced Studies in Science and Technology Policy, a private nonpartisan research organization.

FISA [the Foreign Intelligence Surveillance Act of 1978] should be amended as it is no longer adequate either to enable legitimate foreign intelligence activity or to protect privacy and civil liberties. FISA simply did not anticipate the nature of the current threat to national security from transnational terrorism, nor did it anticipate the development of global communication networks or advanced technical methods for intelligence gathering. Because of technology developments unanticipated in 1978, FISA warrant and procedural re quirements are now being triggered in circumstances not originally intended to be covered by FISA and for which such procedures were not designed and are not well-suited.

The current public debate over FISA modernization is needlessly polarized because of a failure to adequately address directly the fundamental political and policy challenges resulting from this blurring of the previously clear demarcation between reactive law enforcement–derived policies governing the use of targeted "wiretaps" to monitor communications of known persons in the United States pursuant to warrants issued on a prior showing of probable cause on the one hand, and preemptive national security strategies that rely on "signals intelligence" (activity not directed at targeted individuals in the United States but rather at finding information with foreign intelligence value for counterterrorism or counterproliferation purposes from monitoring foreign intelligence

K. A. Taipale, statement for the record, U.S. Senate Select Committee on Intelligence hearing, May 1, 2007, pp. 1–14. Reproduced by permission.

channels or targets, including their international communications to and from the United States) to identify and preempt unknown threats on the other. . . .

While the administration's proposed amendments address the same problems with FISA that we have previously identified—and we generally support the effort to modernize FISA—we would prefer to see an additional statutory authorization or oversight mechanism specifically designed to provide additional privacy and civil liberties protection (through specific authorities, oversight, or review) for situations in which either programmatic or foreign-targeted signals intelligence activities are likely to have a significant impact on persons in the United States. Thus, we urge that the Committee, the Congress, and the administration consider the issues discussed below.

Changes in Technology Challenge the Existing FISA Framework

When FISA was enacted in 1978 it was intended only to cover targeted foreign intelligence interceptions of domestic communications within the United States. It was specifically not intended to cover non-targeted signals intelligence activities to collect foreign intelligence (nor communications intercepted incidental to surveillance targeting a foreign intelligence target not itself subject to FISA). The exclusion of National Security Agency ("NSA") signals intelligence activities, including activities directed at intercepting international communications, was explicitly acknowledged at the time. . . .

Certain . . . "foreign" activities increasingly infringe on the legitimate privacy expectations of persons in the U.S. in ways and degrees not previously contemplated.

The legislative history is replete with references acknowledging Congressional awareness of ongoing signals intelligence activities relating to international communications then being conducted by the NSA (including "sweeping" interceptions of communications where one end was in the United States) and makes it clear that it was not contemplated that such activity was to be subject to FISA warrant or procedural requirements.

Indeed, the differing statutory standards enacted in FISA for "wire" and "radio" intercepts, and for interceptions conducted "within the United States" and abroad, were designed specifically as statutory mechanisms to preserve the distinction between signals intelligence not subject to FISA and targeted domestic activity that was to be its domain.

Thirty years ago when FISA was being drafted these technical distinctions based on place or method served to distinguish signals intelligence from targeted "wiretapping" and made perfect sense given the then prevalent practices and technologies. Signals intelligence activities at that time were primarily being conducted by foreign intelligence agencies like the NSA through interception of satellite or microwave transmissions (i.e., "radio") that could be intercepted from abroad (even when they had one "end" in the United States), and targeted interceptions of specific communications of known persons were generally being conducted by law enforcement or counterintelligence agencies like the FBI using a "wiretap or microphone" on circuit-based "wire" transmissions within the United States. FISA was intended to cover the latter and designed to exclude the former.

Unfortunately, these outdated technical distinctions are now inadequate to address certain technology developments that have occurred since the enactment of FISA, including the transition from circuit-based communications to packet-based communications; the globalization of communications infrastructure; and the development of automated monitoring techniques, including data mining and traffic analysis.

Because of these technology developments, much legitimate foreign signals intelligence activity directed at finding signals of interest (that is, activity not directed at targeted individuals in the United States but rather at finding information with foreign intelligence value for counterterrorism or counter-proliferation purposes from monitoring legitimate foreign intelligence channels or targets, including their international communications to and from the United States) can no longer be conducted within the framework envisioned by FISA. Activities previously accomplished by radio interceptions or conducted abroad (and intentionally excluded from FISA procedures) are increasingly only possible through interceptions conducted at communication switches within the United States (including "transit intercepts" of wholly foreign communications) or at switches or fiber optic cable repeaters that carry significant U.S. person or domestic traffic as well (resulting in the "substantial likelihood" of collateral intercepts), thus, potentially triggering FISA and its procedural requirements in circumstances that were not contemplated at enactment. . . .

Our system of government works best, and public confidence is best maintained, only when the branches of government work together in consensus.

Preemption, Not Technology, Poses the More Difficult Policy Problem

The fundamental challenge to existing law and policy, however, is not technological—if it were, resolution might be more easily accomplished. The real challenge arises from the need to pursue preemptive strategies against certain potentially catastrophic threats from transnational terrorism and nuclear weapons proliferation that in part necessitate using electronic surveillance methods that were not originally intended to be covered by FISA or related warrant procedures (and that don't easily lend themselves to such practices) but that increasingly affect the privacy and civil liberties interests of persons in the United States.

The challenge is in crafting a new framework—one that is both enabling of legitimate foreign intelligence activities and yet protective of privacy and civil liberties—to govern the use of signals intelligence methods (particularly, those methods that were originally not intended to be subject to FISA and for which the existing FISA procedures are not well-suited) against new national security threats when these uses increasingly impact the same privacy and civil liberties interests that FISA *was* originally intended to address.

The policy conundrum is in reconciling the rigid law enforcement-derived policies and procedures intended to govern the use of electronic surveillance technologies to monitor the activities of known subjects with the more amorphous foreign intelligence and national security strategies needed to identify previously unknown threats (in order to develop the kind of actionable intelligence necessary for preemption). These activities were previously subject to disparate and often conflicting policy regimes—the former subject to formal judicial warrant procedures under FISA and the latter at the sole discretion of the executive with little oversight or review.

The Administration's Proposals

The proposed Foreign Intelligence Surveillance Modernization Act of 2007 ("FISMA") would amend FISA to exclude most foreign and international signals intelligence activity from triggering FISA warrant requirements by simplifying the definition of "electronic surveillance" for purposes of the statute to interceptions (1) intentionally targeting a particular, known person reasonably believed to be in the United States, or (2) intentionally acquiring the contents of communications when all parties are reasonably believed to be in the United States. The effect of these changes would be to exclude any non-targeted interception of international communications from FISA or its warrant requirements even if one party to the communication was in the United States.

Although it can be argued persuasively that such a proposal merely updates—in a way no longer dependent on outdated technical distinctions—the original legislative intention for FISA to not cover these kinds of activities, in our view it fails to acknowledge the political reality that certain of these "foreign" activities increasingly infringe on the legitimate privacy expectations of persons in the U.S. in ways and degrees not previously contemplated and, therefore, as a *policy* matter, certain of these activities with the potential for significant domestic impact may now require some form of explicit statutory authorization and oversight mechanism external to the executive branch to create political consensus, reassure the public, and provide democratic accountability.

If the existing FISA warrant procedures were to be strictly applied to all foreign intelligence activities then no useful signals intelligence activity of any kind would be possible.

Thus, regardless of whether the executive indeed has inherent authority to conduct foreign intelligence surveillance activities—including those that intercept international communications to and from the United States—without such explicit statutory authority or oversight, our system of government works best, and public confidence is best maintained, only when the branches of government work together in consensus and the broad parameters of procedural due process protections are publicly debated and agreed. . . .

Requiring Traditional FISA Warrants for Signals Intelligence Is Unworkable

Many critics of the administration's proposed amendments concede that changes in technology have undermined the existing FISA framework. However, they argue that rather than excluding non-targeted or foreign intelligence activities from FISA as proposed by the administration, that these technology developments justify extending existing FISA warrant requirements to all electronic surveillance activities in which U.S. person or domestic communications are likely to be intercepted, even if no U.S. person or communication is targeted and the communication is merely acquired incidental to the targeting of legitimate foreign intelligence targets. But, in doing so they ignore the fundamentally different requirements and circumstances of non-targeted or foreign signals intelligence and targeted domestic wiretaps.

If the existing FISA warrant procedures were to be strictly applied to all foreign intelligence activities then no useful signals intelligence activity of any kind would be possible—there would simply be no procedure under which electronic signals intelligence could be employed to uncover unknown connections or threats from persons in the United States communicating or conspiring with known al Qa'ida or affiliated operatives. Such an outcome would, of course, have significant national security ramifications. In any case, there is no constitutional requirement for warrants in these circumstances. . . .

The problem with the FISA procedures as currently constituted is that FISA provides only a single binary *a priori* threshold for authorizing any electronic interception—probable cause that the target is an agent of a foreign power. Unfortunately, even extensive contact with a known terrorist may not be procedurally sufficient to satisfy the current statutory requirements for a FISA warrant, and, more importantly, such contacts may only be discoverable through non-targeted or foreign directed signals intelligence activities in the first place. . . .

Non-content Transactional Data

Although FISA currently has provisions for authorizing the targeted collection of non-content information—the FISA pen register and trap-and-trace provisions—it does not provide any procedures for authorizing even specific but non-targeted traffic or link analysis that may be required—and wholly reasonable—in the context of foreign signals intelligence to identify certain connections or threats.

For example, known patterns of terrorist communications can be identified and used to uncover other unknown but indirectly related terrorists or terrorist activity. Thus, for instance, in the immediate aftermath of 9/11 the FBI determined that the leaders of the 19 hijackers had made 206 international telephone calls to specific locations in Saudi Arabia, Syria, and Germany. It is believed that in order to determine whether any other unknown persons—so-called sleeper cells—in the United States might have been in communication with the same pattern of foreign correspondents the NSA analyzed Call Data Records (CDRs) of international and domestic phone calls obtained from the major U.S. telecommunication companies.

It is well settled law that dialing or signaling information is entitled to lesser constitutional protection from disclosure than is content.

Undertaking such an analysis seems reasonable, particularly in the circumstances immediately following 9/11, yet FISA and existing procedures do not provide *any* approval or review mechanism for determining such reasonableness or for authorizing or governing such activity because FISA simply did not contemplate the current need for approval of specific—but non-targeted—pattern-based data searches or surveillance.

Further, while it is well settled law that dialing or signaling information is entitled to lesser constitutional protection from disclosure than is content, FISA as currently enacted is somewhat confusingly inconsistent about how such information is to be treated even in cases of targeted acquisition. FISA currently defines "content" to include "the identity of the parties to such communication or the existence" of the communication (*i.e..*, transactional information) but it also authorizes orders for pen registers and trap-and-trace devices to collect such information under a lesser standard than the statute requires for "content" intercepts.

The administration's FISA modernization proposals would address both the failure to anticipate the need for non-targeted traffic analysis and the inconsistency in statutory language for targeted collection by changing the definition of content to exclude transaction data and by simplifying the definition of "electronic surveillance" to only cover content interception.

Again, while there is a strong case that the administration proposal is consistent with existing law and the original intent of FISA, nevertheless—for the same reasons set forth above regarding programmatic approval of content based signals intelligence—some statutory procedure to authorize and approve directed traffic or link analysis of transactional communication records where there is a significant impact on U.S. persons or domestic communications seems desirable as a matter of public policy.

FISA as currently enacted fails to adequately enable legitimate and necessary foreign intelligence surveillance activity or to adequately protect privacy and civil liberties.

The same kind of approval mechanisms discussed above for programmatic approvals might be applicable in these circumstances as well, recognizing, of course, that approvals for these activities should be subject to a lesser standard than those involving content, consistent with existing law.

FISA Must Be Updated

FISA as currently enacted fails to adequately enable legitimate and necessary foreign intelligence surveillance activity or to adequately protect privacy and civil liberties.

The administration is seeking to explicitly exclude from FISA statutory requirements those non-targeted or foreign signals intelligence activities that were not originally intended to be included in the FISA regime and that don't fit easily within its existing framework. Although we agree that this proposal is wholly consistent with the original intent of FISA, we are concerned that these kinds of activities increasingly impact the same domestic privacy and civil liberties interests that the political compromise leading to FISA was intended to address.

On the other hand, the critics of the administration's proposals are arguing simply to extend ill-suited FISA warrant procedures over activities that have different requirements and considerations than those for which FISA was designed and enacted. Force fitting these existing procedures to cover all signals intelligence activities that may affect U.S. persons is simply unworkable, is not constitutionally required, and would severely frustrate the ability to gather foreign intelligence information vital to the national security and interests of the United States.

The Center for Advanced Studies urges Congress to consider an adaptive legislative framework that will enable legitimate foreign intelligence activities while still protecting privacy and civil liberties; and that explicitly recognizes the different requirements and circumstances of signals intelligence and targeted wiretaps.

FISA . . . is wholly ineffective for enabling or constraining the use of foreign signals intelligence to help identify threats in the first place.

We urge Congress to consider enacting an institutional mechanism for the programmatic approval, oversight, and review of legitimate foreign signals intelligence activity or programs where such activity is likely to have substantial impact on domestic privacy or civil liberties interests, as well as to provide some explicit guidelines governing how information derived from such programs can be reasonably used to protect the national security of the United States while still protecting privacy and civil liberties consistent with existing laws.

FISA as currently constituted is viable only for monitoring the activities of known agents of a foreign power but it is wholly ineffective for enabling or constraining the use of foreign signals intelligence to help identify threats in the first place or otherwise gather signals with foreign intelligence value to the United States. FISA must be updated to address these failures in order to protect both national security and individual freedom. Both values are indispensable and must be reconciled.

The Proposed Amendment to the FISA Would Pardon Telecommunications Companies that Broke the Law

Caroline Frederickson

Caroline Frederickson is the director of the American Civil Liberties Union's Washington Legislative Office.

On behalf of the American Civil Liberties Union, and its hundreds of thousands of activists and members, and fifty-three affiliates nationwide, we urge you in the strongest terms to oppose legislation drafted by the Department of Justice ("DOJ") that would effectively pardon telecommunication companies for illegal behavior over the last five years and re-write the Foreign Intelligence Surveillance Act ("FISA") to facilitate further warrantless surveillance on American soil.

Only a few short weeks ago this Congress was finally informed about the DOJ's use of National Security Letters ("NSLs") and found that this power—no longer limited to collecting information on terrorists—is being abused to collect vast amounts of data on innocent Americans that is stored indefinitely in massive federal databases accessible by tens of thousands of users. Instead of contemplating ways to exponentially increase those powers, this Congress should be figuring out ways to rein them in, protect constitutional rights, and focus our antiterrorism resources on suspected terrorists.

While the Administration claims that the changes it proposes to FISA would "modernize" it, they would better be described as changes to gut the judicial oversight mechanisms carefully crafted to prevent abuse, while expanding the uni-

Caroline Frederickson, "Statement Submitted to the Select Committee on Intelligence, U.S. Senate," American Civil Liberties Union (ACLU), May 1, 2007. Reproduced by permission.

verse of communications that can be intercepted under FISA. They would allow the intelligence community to return to the tarnished practices of the 1970's and earlier, when warrants were largely optional and abusive spying was not limited to subjects who had done something wrong. In fact, despite numerous hearings about "modernization" and "technology neutrality" over the last year, the Administration has not publicly provided Congress with a single example of how current standards in FISA have either prevented the intelligence community from using new technologies or proven unworkable for the personnel tasked with following them. Congress should not approve sweeping new authorities without such a showing by the Administration.

Granting Immunity to the Companies That Facilitated Illegal Spying Is Inappropriate

We are disappointed and very concerned that the first hearing in this Congress to address five years of illegal spying would consider a legislative, congressional pardon for the telecommunication companies that broke the law. Congress' priority should be a full and public airing of the government's illegal spying, including determining exactly how many people the government and telecommunications companies spied on for five years and what is now being done with records of those phone calls; holding those who broke the law responsible; and then fashioning a response to make sure these grave violations of privacy never happen again.

The Administration's proposed bill is objectionable because it eliminates independent court review of the Administration's past and future spying and eavesdropping requests.

This Committee should be holding a hearing to determine how to contract, rather than expand, the government's illegal spying to bring it into conformity with the law and Constitution; yet the Administration's proposed bill proposes an unwise new power grab. For example, sections 408 and 411 attempt to terminate all pending and future actions against the NSA's warrantless wiretapping in any court anywhere, except for a FISA court whose judges are handpicked by the Chief Justice. The US District Court in the Eastern District of Michigan recently ruled that the president's program to wiretap Americans without warrants is illegal and unconstitutional. The Administration, having lost in one forum, asks Congress to give it a new one.

The Administration's proposed bill is objectionable because it eliminates independent court review of the Administration's past and future spying and eavesdropping requests. The proposed bill would allow the administration to rip that case from that court's jurisdiction, and ship other federal and state court challenges off for secret hearings and proceedings before the FISA Court of Review, which has handled only one case in nearly 30 years. And, only the government would be allowed to appeal to the U.S. Supreme Court to seek review of any adverse ruling by that Court. The bill abrogates rights granted under state law as well, by stopping state law enforcement and regulatory agencies from enforcing local consumer privacy laws that may offer more protection than federal law. Beyond the mandatory transfer provision, the bill allows companies to assert immunity for complying with secret requests of the AG [Attorney General] under provisions that state that:

> No action shall lie or be maintained in any court, and no penalty, sanction or other form of remedy or relief shall be imposed by any court or any other body, against any person for the alleged provision to an element of the intelligence community of any information (including records or other information pertaining to a customer), facilities or any other

form of assistance during the period of time beginning on September 11, 2001, and ending on the date that is the effective date of this Act...

This rush to retroactive immunity for an entire industry in the absence of full and thorough airing of the facts is unprecedented.

This exemption is both overbroad and unwise.

If Congress grants these companies immunity for violating longstanding privacy laws, what incentive will they have to follow them in the future? Without consequences, these laws ring hollow, and end up being a mere suggestion instead of a mandate or bright line requirement. For nearly 30 years, FISA has included a clear liability and immunity scheme that creates bright lines for telecommunication companies: if they turn over private information in response to a legal demand from the government, they are 100 percent immune from any liability. However, if they cut a side deal with the executive branch in an attempt to bypass the duly enacted laws of this Congress, they are liable to the consumers whose privacy they have betrayed. If our government wants to "improv[e] the way the United States does business with communications providers," as the DOJ claims on the fact sheet it conveyed to Congress with its legislative proposal, it should return to the days of clear cut requirements, instead of enticing those providers to break the law with the promise of a congressional pardon after the fact.

Finally, this rush to retroactive immunity for an entire industry in the absence of full and thorough airing of the facts is unprecedented. Numerous leaders in this Congress have promised to investigate the President's illegal Terrorist Surveillance Program. It is highly unlikely those investigations will yield any useful information if Congress starts the process giving the companies a get out of jail free card.

Changing Technical Definitions in FISA to Undercut the Warrant Requirement of the Fourth Amendment

Sections 401 and 402 of the proposed Administration bill alter FISA's current definitions of "electronic surveillance" to greatly reduce the number and scope of spying activities that are subject to court review. The DOJ's Office of Public Policy claims these changes are necessary "to account for the sweeping changes in telecommunications technology that have taken place." This includes making FISA "technology neutral" by deleting the longstanding requirement that all wire communications into and out of the U.S. are accessed only on the basis of a warrant.

These changes have absolutely nothing to do with "modernizing" FISA—rather, they substantially and unconstitutionally declare whole categories of communications exempt from the warrant requirement, namely, 1) international phone calls, even when made in the U.S. by a U.S. person, and 2) phone calls collected as a part of a general dragnet, as long as no one U.S. person was targeted. Technology may have changed, but the Fourth Amendment has not. Except for a few very narrow circumstances, warrants are required to listen to phone calls or otherwise access the content of a communication and we ask this committee to make sure that requirement remains a cornerstone of FISA.

This draft proposal would also allow the NSA to acquire Americans' private e-mail messages.

The Justice Department has claimed that this proposal restores the "original intent" of the law but the legislative history makes clear that Congress intended FISA to prevent the National Security Agency ("NSA") from engaging in just the sort of electronic dragnet this bill permits. The Church Committee's discovery that the NSA was improperly monitoring millions of international telegrams to and from Americans and U.S. businesses through "Operation Shamrock" led a bipartisan coalition in Congress to enact FISA to prevent future presidents from intercepting the "international communications of American citizens whose privacy ought to be protected under the Constitution" ever again. See Book III of the Final Report on Intelligence Activities and the Rights of Americans, Apr. 23, 1976, at pp. 735–36.

This draft proposal would also allow the NSA to acquire Americans' private e-mail messages if the government says it does not know that "the sender and all intended recipients are located within" the U.S. This provision would authorize the NSA to vacuum up all of the international emails of Americans. The NSA would likely capture purely domestic e-mails in this program as well because, as Central Intelligence Agency Director General Michael Hayden said, "there are no zip codes on the world wide web." For example, if an American in New York City sends an email to his sister in San Francisco, that communication could be intercepted without a warrant because it went through Canada. This bill would allow the NSA to keep these "accidentally" captured communications. Once "lawfully" acquired under this authority, the administration could—and most likely already does—interpret the statute to allow the NSA to target particular Americans' communications from such a dragnet for data mining, analysis, or dissemination. Because this activity is not considered "electronic surveillance" under the new language proposed in this bill, a substantial number of innocent Americans' private conversations would be exempt from the oversight of the court and congressional reporting. While the bill retains FISA's minimization rules, those rules only apply to "electronic surveillance" which is redefined in this draft bill to exclude innocent Americans' international conversations and e-mails. Thus, this supposed protection is illusory.

The proposal also amends FISA to require a warrant only when a surveillance device acquires conversations by "intentionally directing the surveillance" at a specific U.S. person. Under the Justice Department's draft bill, if the NSA's surveillance devices—as distinguished from its data mining devices— are directed at wholly domestic conversations but not at a specific American, no warrant need be sought. FISA's targeting language is a shield against sweeping up the conversations of innocent Americans. The proposed language turns this into a sword to cut down statutory protections for our Fourth Amendment rights.

Stripping Non-citizens—and Anyone Who Comes into Contact with Them— of the Protection of a Warrant

Section 402 greatly reduces the protection against government spying on non-U.S. persons and puts at risk the privacy of any U.S. persons who may come into contact with them. Current law has a narrow exception to the warrant requirement that allows the Attorney General to issue wiretap orders for 1) communications that are exclusively between foreign powers, such as contact between embassies and foreign countries, or 2) technical intelligence from property under the exclusive control of a foreign power, when either of these activities has "no substantial likelihood that the surveillance will acquire the contents of any communication to which a United States person is a party." Section 402 strips both the requirement that communications or technical intelligence be exclusively between or on the property of a foreign power, and the requirement that there be no substantial likelihood that a U.S. person be caught up in the surveillance. This greatly increases the chances, and in fact expressly allows, that a U.S. person may have his or her communications scooped up in surveillance of foreign powers.

This bill even expands the definition of "agent of a foreign power" to include anyone in the U.S. who is not a citizen, lawful permanent resident or company incorporated in the U.S. who "is expected to possess, control, transmit or receive foreign intelligence information" in the U.S. This is dangerous because FISA's definition of "foreign intelligence" is not limited to international terrorism but includes information about the "national defense," "security," or "conduct of the foreign affairs" of the U.S., which has been construed to include trade matters. All foreign journalism and foreign-owned media companies, financial institutions, airlines, telecommunications companies, or Internet Service Providers (ISPs) could be considered "agents of a foreign power" whose communications could be seized without any suspicion of wrongdoing, just because they all can reasonably be expected to "possess," "transmit" and "receive" foreign intelligence information within the United States. Communications of many foreign businesses in the U.S. transmit or hold information that involves foreign affairs, particularly foreign media and financial institutions. All the Administration would have to show to get a FISA order to search or wiretap these entities for an entire year is that these entities possess such information, not that they have done or are expected to do anything improper. . . .

A number of other provisions in this proposed bill appear to have no purpose other than to reduce the checks and balances in FISA. Section 405 extends the maximum time period for a FISA warrant for a non-U.S. citizen from 120 days to one year, and extends the duration of emergency wiretap orders that allow the government to surveil suspects without prior judicial review from 72 hours to one week. Section 410 extends the period of emergency trap and trace orders from 48 hours to one week. Again, the Administration has provided no evidence that the current time limits are unworkable. While the Justice Department has requested "flexibility," and justifies less court review under the guise of saving time, periodic and timely review of orders is necessary to ensure that the government does not continue spying on people in the absence of some evidence that the person is a terrorist. . . .

The proposed amendments to FISA do not "modernize" intelligence-gathering activities. They simply declare certain communications outside of the warrant requirement and reduce judicial oversight, in violation of the Fourth Amendment. In light of recent revelations that the government is gravely abusing the authorities it already has, allowing this exponential increase in spying authority would not only be unconstitutional, but irresponsible. We urge you to resist any such expansion.

The Proposed Amendment to the FISA Would Deprive Americans of the Right to Communicate Privately

Kevin S. Bankston

Kevin S. Bankston is a staff attorney for the Electronic Freedom Foundation.

EFF [the Electronic Frontier Foundation] is a non-profit, member-supported public interest organization dedicated to protecting privacy and free speech in the digital age. As part of that mission, EFF is representing current and former residential customers of AT&T in a civil action against that company for its alleged cooperation in the National Security Agency's warrantless dragnet surveillance of its customers' telephone calls and Internet communications. Just as Congress' laws prohibiting warrantless electronic surveillance bind the government, so too do they bind those telecommunications carriers that are entrusted with transmitting Americans' private communications. As Congress recognized when it provided civil causes of action against communications providers that violate that trust, the ability to maintain such lawsuits is a key check against illegal collaborations between the Executive and those that control access to our national telecommunications infrastructure.

The amendments to FISA currently proposed by the Administration threaten to deprive our plaintiffs of their day in court, and to deprive all Americans of their right to communicate privately. That proposal, far from "modernizing" the law, would gut the long-standing checks and balances that

Kevin S. Bankston, "Testimony before the Select Committee on Intelligence, U.S. Senate," Electronic Frontier Foundation, May 1, 2007, pp. 5–10. www.eff.org. Reproduced by permission.

Congress established to rein in the Executive's ability to spy on Americans. It would shield surveillance conducted in the name of national security from meaningful judicial scrutiny, and unjustifiably provide blanket immunity for illegal surveillance conducted since September 11, 2001—surveillance that Congress has not yet even investigated, and which appears to go far beyond the narrow "Terrorist Surveillance Program" admitted to by the President.

[The proposed amendment] could essentially provide the Attorney General with a stack of blank "get out of jail free" cards for both government agents and telecommunications carriers.

Unfortunately, this Administration has squandered the people's trust over the past five years, flagrantly ignoring FISA's requirements by wiretapping Americans without warrants and routinely abusing its authority under the USA PATRIOT Act to obtain Americans' private records. It can no longer be given the benefit of the doubt by Congress in these matters. When a large margin of Americans believe that the President has failed to properly balance the preservation of civil liberties against national security concerns, what is most needed is vigorous investigation and oversight by Congress and the Courts—not a statutory blank check granting the Executive even greater surveillance authority, nor a pardon for government agents and telecommunications companies that have violated the law in the past. The Administration and the telephone companies must understand that they cannot ignore the statutes passed by Congress and then simply demand amnesty when caught in the act.

Other commentators have already explained at length how passage of the Administration's proposal as a whole would dangerously and unjustifiably expand the Executive's surveillance powers. Therefore, this statement will focus on those provisions that would most directly impact pending lawsuits against the government and telecommunications carriers for their illegal collaboration in the surveillance of Americans' private communications. . . .

Taken together, these provisions represent a concerted attack on the rights of Americans to seek redress when subjected to illegal surveillance, and are an obvious attempt to shield the Administration and its collaborators against judicial inquiry into their illegal surveillance activities since 9/11.

Blanket Immunity for Illegal Surveillance

The Administration has repeatedly assured Congress and the public that its warrantless surveillance of Americans is fully consistent with the law. Those claims ring hollow, however, when read in conjunction with Section 408 of its proposal. With Section 408, the Administration seeks to provide blanket immunity against liability to any person who has assisted in any government surveillance activity that the Attorney General or his designee claims was undertaken in the name of anti-terrorism. The Administration's bid for such immunity essentially concedes the weakness of its legal arguments in support of warrantless surveillance, arguments that it clearly hopes to insulate from judicial scrutiny.

Specifically, the breathtakingly broad terms of Section 408 provide that:

> Notwithstanding any other law, and in addition to the immunities, privileges, and defenses provided by any other source of law, no action shall lie or be maintained in any court, and no penalty, sanction, or other form of remedy or relief shall be imposed by any court or any other body, against any person for the alleged provision to an element of the intelligence community of any information (including records or other information pertaining to a customer), facilities, or any other form of assistance, during the period of time beginning on September 11, 2001, and ending on the

date that is the effective date of this Act, in connection with any alleged classified communications intelligence activity that the Attorney General or a designee of the Attorney General certifies, in a manner consistent with the protection of State secrets, is, was, would be, or would have been intended to protect the United States from a terrorist attack. This section shall apply to all actions, claims, or proceedings pending on or after the effective date of this Act.

As an initial matter, this provision does not just protect telecommunications carriers. Rather, it appears designed to also shield *the government itself* against any lawsuit concerning its "classified communications intelligence activit[ies]" since 9/11. In particular, the proposed immunity would reach any "person" as defined at 18 U.S.C. § 2510(6), *i.e.*, "any employee, or agent of the United States or any State or political subdivision thereof, and any individual, partnership, association, joint stock company, trust, or corporation."

Congress must not legislate in the dark, particularly when the rights of so many are at stake.

Furthermore, this provision's language is not expressly limited to immunity from civil liability. Instead, it seeks to prevent the imposition of *any* "penalty, sanction, or other form of remedy or relief" in *any* legal action in *any* court. Such expansive language could be read to preclude even criminal prosecution. Therefore Section 408 could essentially provide the Attorney General with a stack of blank "get out of jail free" cards for both government agents and telecommunications carriers, representing a complete abandonment of the rule of law when it comes to government surveillance conducted in the name of national security.

The Scope of Misconduct Is Unknown

That Congress might consider such unprecedented blanket immunity for government agents and the telecommunications carriers that illegally assisted them is all the more shocking considering that neither Congress nor the public even knows what conduct it would be immunizing. Senator Arlen Specter has aptly described Section 408 as "a pig in the poke" since "there has never been a statement from the administration as to what these companies have done." Nor has the Administration come clean about its own conduct, publicly admitting only to the purportedly narrow "Terrorist Surveillance Program" described by the President even as news reports and whistle-blower evidence indicate a much broader program.

Congress must not legislate in the dark, particularly when the rights of so many are at stake. Indeed, it would be unwise for Congress to consider *any* kind of immunity when it has yet to investigate the scope and legality of the Administration's conduct. How many Americans have had their privacy violated? How did telecommunications carriers assist in those violations of privacy, and what were they given in return? Congress must conduct a full investigation to uncover the answers to those questions. The public and its elected representatives deserve a full accounting of the Administration's illegal surveillance activities and the telecommunications carriers' participation in that surveillance. Such a full accounting is unlikely ever to occur if every person involved has already been granted a no-strings-attached legislative pardon.

> *Telecommunications carriers' adherence to the law is the biggest practical check that we have against illegal government surveillance.*

In addition to doing its job by investigating how the Administration has abused its surveillance power since 9/11, Congress should allow the courts to do *their* job by allowing them to adjudicate the legality of that surveillance and the telephone companies' participation in it. The telecommunications industry appears to have assisted the Administration in the greatest mass privacy invasion ever perpetrated on the American people. Americans are entitled to discover the extent to which their privacy was violated and to have a court decide whether the law was broken. Immunity would short-circuit this judicial process, potentially eliminating the courts as a meaningful check on illegal collaboration between telecommunications carriers and the Executive Branch.

Increased Risk of Illegal Collaborations

Not only is Section 408 designed to ensure that past surveillance by the Administration and its collaborators in the telecommunications industry remains shrouded in secrecy and shielded from judicial review, it would also dangerously increase the risk of *future* illegal collaborations between government and communications providers. Telecommunications carriers' adherence to the law is the biggest practical check that we have against illegal government surveillance. Giving blanket immunity to those carriers, which are the only entities standing between the privacy of countless innocent Americans and government overreaching, sets a dangerous precedent. Section 408 threatens to make Congress' laws a dead letter, eliminated by secret meetings between telecommunications executives and government agents, greased by the promise of similar grants of immunity in the future. There is no reason for Congress to take that risk, as federal law already provides legal protections that adequately protect carriers' good faith cooperation in response to lawful requests by the government.

Instead, in order to fully hold accountable those telecommunications carriers that broke the law and to protect against future law-breaking, Congress should allow those customers whose privacy has been violated to press for the remedies to which they are entitled under statute. Congress rightly established strong civil penalties for violation of FISA and its fellow surveillance statutes, and EFF strongly opposes any legislation that would deprive its clients or any other Americans of the remedies to which they are entitled. Congress' carefully crafted penalties were meant to serve as a strong disincentive against illegal assistance in government surveillance, and to cast them aside now would send a dangerous message: that when the government comes calling and uses the magic words "national security" or "terrorism," communications providers should feel free to ignore the law.

[Carriers] must be held to account if we are to prevent secret and unchecked access to the telecommunications networks that carry all of our most private communications.

Finally, to the extent that Congress is concerned by the potential economic impact of such liability on America's telecommunications industry, such concern is wholly premature. Although EFF is confident that its clients will prevail in their current lawsuit against AT&T, that case and other lawsuits against those companies accused of assisting in the Administration's illegal surveillance are still in their early stages. Assuming that the plaintiffs in those suits will ultimately prevail, any award of money damages is likely many years away. Congress should at least allow those cases to continue so that the full scope and legality of the companies' conduct may be discovered and litigated. Then, when the final day of reckoning for the phone companies at last approaches, Congress will have the benefit of a fully developed judicial record to assist it in considering whether the damages to be imposed would be too much—or not nearly enough.

In conclusion, rather than bowing to the Administration's wholly unjustified proposal of blanket immunity, Congress should instead stick to the law that is already on the books. Existing law already strikes a reasonable and bright-line balance between the government's need for industry cooperation in lawful surveillance and the public's need for accountability when industry fails to demand appropriate legal process. The Administration is correct that "companies that cooperate with the Government in the war on terror" deserve "our appreciation and protection"—when they do so lawfully. But they deserve neither appreciation nor protection when they break the law and violate the trust of their customers, whether under the claim of national security or otherwise. To the contrary, they deserve to be held to account for their conduct, and indeed must be held to account if we are to prevent secret and unchecked access to the telecommunications networks that carry all of our most private communications.

New Technologies Demand Stronger, Not Weaker, Privacy Protection

James X. Dempsey

James X. Dempsey is the policy director of the Center for Democracy and Technology, a nonprofit public policy organization.

On April 13 [2007], the Administration offered a bill to make major amendments to FISA [the Foreign Intelligence Surveillance Act of 1978]. The bill is cloaked in the rhetoric of modernization, but it would turn back the clock to an era of unchecked surveillance of the communications of US citizens, permitting the [National Security Agency] NSA's vacuum cleaners to be used on all international calls and email of US citizens without court order. . . .

Today, interception of communications into and out of the U.S. is likely to pick up the communications of many average American citizens.

Of course, technology has changed since FISA was adopted in 1978, but some of those changes have made snooping easier, and in aggregate they have increased the amount of information about our daily lives that is available electronically to the government, thereby requiring stronger, not weaker privacy protections.

The Administration's bill would go in the wrong direction, by permitting the untargeted warrantless surveillance of all international communications of US citizens. The most important part of the bill would change FISA's definition of "electronic surveillance" to say, in Alice in Wonderland fashion,

James X. Dempsey, testimony before the Select Committee on Intelligence, U.S. Senate, May 1, 2007, pp. 1–15. Reproduced by permission.

that the sweeping collection of the international phone calls, email and other communications of American citizens is not "electronic surveillance" and therefore does not require a court order. . . .

FISA may need to be updated, but the first step is for the Administration to clearly explain on the public record why FISA is inadequate, which it has failed to do. So far, to the extent that the Administration has actually described issues with FISA, they are ones that could be addressed with much narrower changes. And any changes to FISA should include increased privacy protections, which are clearly needed.

The Administration's proposal is an exercise in cherry-picking: Arguing that FISA is outdated, and claiming to seek consistency and technology neutrality, the Administration proposes to change only aspects of FISA that serve as checks upon its discretion. The Administration accepts unquestioningly those elements of FISA that accord it broad latitude. The result would be a law that is still inconsistent and outdated, but far less protective of the rights of Americans. If there is truly a need to revise FISA, then the reconsideration of Congress' 1978 choices must proceed systematically, not on the basis of a one-sided selectivity. As we explain below, careful consideration should be given to two fundamental elements of FISA: its distinction between wire and radio communications and its distinction between targeted and untargeted surveillance. . . .

Changes in Technology Require Stronger, Not Weaker, Standards

The Administration justifies its bill largely on the ground that changes in technology have made FISA outdated. Of course, technology has changed since 1978, but that begs the question of whether FISA should be weakened in response. The Administration never actually explains what technology changes have taken place since 1978, nor does it explain why any such changes justify weakening FISA.

A balanced analysis would show that various technological changes since 1978 require stronger rather than weaker FISA standards.

Everything we know about the digital revolution indicates that, on balance, it has been a windfall for the snoopers.

Perhaps the major change since 1978 that affects FISA is the globalization of personal and economic life, paralleled by the central role of global electronic communications networks in commerce, interpersonal relationships, and the full range of human pursuits. In 1978, it was a rarity for an American citizen to make an international phone call or send an international telegram. In 1978, the signals intelligence activities of the National Security Agency collected some international calls of Americans, but it was pretty rare. Today, interception of communications into and out of the US is likely to pick up the communications of many average American citizens and permanent resident aliens, who are far more likely than in 1978 to have legitimate business dealings overseas or to use the Internet and telephone to keep in touch with relatives overseas. The parent calling her daughter during her junior year abroad, the Chicago lawyer talking to his partner in Brussels, and the small Texas manufacturer with a parts supplier in Vietnam are all entitled to a reasonable expectation of privacy in their international communications. Far more than in 1978, signals intelligence activity directed at communications entering and leaving the United States is likely to interfere with the privacy of Americans, which means that it must be carefully controlled.

Secondly, while there has been a huge increase in the volume of international communications, there have also been huge increases in computer processing power, making it possible for the government to process more data than ever before. Everything we know about the digital revolution indicates that, on balance, it has been a windfall for the snoopers: More electronic information than ever before is available to the government, and the government's ability to process that information is exponentially greater than ever before. The intelligence agencies are in constant danger of drowning in this information, but they are also constantly improving their processing and analytic capabilities. On balance, the question of volume may be a wash: the agencies have a lot more data to deal with, and they have a lot more ability to handle it. The challenge is daunting, and vital to our national security, but it is hard to see how mere volume justifies lower standards for surveillance of calls to and from Americans in the United States. If anything, the increasing amount of information about our daily lives that is exposed to electronic surveillance calls for stronger, not weaker standards.

A third major technological change is the revolutionary growth of the Internet. Some aspects of the Internet's development, especially the routing of a large percentage of international traffic through the United States, actually make the job of the intelligence agencies much easier in some ways, since they can access foreign-to-foreign communications from US soil. Other aspects of the Internet cited by the Administration—such as General Hayden's assertion that "there are no area codes on the Internet"—may not be entirely accurate and, even if true, require close scrutiny to determine what effect they actually have on electronic surveillance activities carried out in the United States. (FISA only applies to surveillance inside the United States.)

The Shift to Fiber Cables Should Not Lower Privacy Standards

A fourth major change—one alluded to by the Administration—is the shift to fiber cables as the dominant means of long distance and international carriage. As we will discuss below, the government's argument hinges on the fact that Congress, in 1978, deferred regulating NSA's interception of the satellite portion of international voice communications. Now, the Administration is arguing that radio's temporary exemption should be made permanent and extended to wire communications as well. This is an extraordinary argument: Essentially the Administration is claiming that Americans never had a privacy right for their international satellite calls and that now, just as Americans have become dependent on the Internet to participate in the global economy, they should not have a privacy right for international communications carried by wire either. CDT [Center for Democracy and Technology] believes that, if it is time to reconsider FISA's "radio exception," it should be to repeal the exception and extend privacy protections to all of the international communications of Americans, not to eliminate privacy protections across the board.

A growing number of companies are developing tools and services to intercept Internet traffic and other advanced communications.

In addition, the Administration never actually explains why the shift to fiber optics requires a lowering of privacy standards for intercepting the international communications of Americans. The fact that fiber cables are hard to tap into is irrelevant for purposes of FISA, since, as we noted, FISA applies only inside the United States, where the government does not have to tap into the middle of a cable, because it can compel the cooperation of the service provider at the network operator's switching facility. FISA specifically states that a court order, upon request of the government, shall require any communications carrier to provide "forthwith all information, facilities, or technical assistance necessary to accomplish the electronic surveillance."

A fifth technology change merits separate highlighting, and that is the development and deployment of new generations of surveillance-enhancing technology by telephone companies and other communications service providers. Partly, the development of tools to facilitate the interception of advanced technologies is business driven. Network operators need to be able to trace, isolate and analyze communications to manage their networks, for billing purposes, maintenance, quality control, and security. Other developments are driven by intellectual property concerns, as companies develop means of scanning vast data flows looking for copyrighted material.

Another driver has been legislation like CALEA, the Communications Assistance for Law Enforcement Act of 1994, which specifically requires all communications common carriers to design their systems to make them wiretap friendly. European countries have similar (in some cases more onerous) requirements, and both American standards bodies and the European Telecommunications Standards Institute have developed standards to guide equipment developers. In August 2005, the Federal Communications Commission extended CALEA to broadband Internet access providers and providers of interconnected VoIP (Voice over Internet Protocol) providers.

The Administration bill . . . changes the definition of electronic surveillance to exclude . . . the collection of a great deal of information about the communications of US citizens that the average person would call "electronic surveillance."

For these and other reasons, a growing number of companies are developing tools and services to intercept Internet traffic and other advanced communications. . . . The relevance to intelligence agencies of these tools, developed for business or law enforcement purposes, is a question that merits examination. It is sufficient for our purposes here to note that such tools exist, and they provide a counterweight to the Administration's claims that technology has made its task more difficult. The availability of these tools is particularly relevant to FISA, since, as we noted above, FISA applies only in the US, where the government has the legal authority to compel the cooperation of service providers.

The Administration Bill Would Expand Warrantless Surveillance

In order to understand the impact of the Administration bill, it is necessary to appreciate that much of the weight of FISA is carried by its definitions. Most importantly, FISA regulates only "electronic surveillance" as that term is uniquely defined in the Act. If the collection of information fits within the Act's definition of "electronic surveillance," it requires a court order or must fall under one of FISA's exceptions. If the collection of information is *excluded* from the definition of electronic surveillance, then it is not regulated by the Act, and the government can proceed without a court order and without reporting to Congress. Therefore, narrowing the definition of electronic surveillance places more activity outside the judicial and Congressional oversight of the Act.

That is precisely what the Administration bill does: It changes the definition of electronic surveillance to exclude from the Act's coverage the collection of a great deal of information about the communications of US citizens that the average person would call "electronic surveillance." Simply put, the changes sought by Administration would authorize large-scale warrantless surveillance of American citizens and the indefinite retention of citizens' communications for future data-mining. . . .

The bill would permit warrantless surveillance far beyond the President's Terrorist Surveillance Program. Until recently, the Administration consistently argued that it should not need a court order when it is targeting a suspected terrorist overseas calling the US. The problem with the TSP even thus narrowly defined is that, of course, there are two parties to the call, one of whom is in the US and is quite likely a citizen. The person on the phone in the US may be a journalist, an innocent relative, an aid worker, or any other variety of innocent person. Yet under this bill the conversations of those innocent Americans will be intercepted without a warrant. . . .

Under this bill, for the first time ever, NSA would be able to train its vacuum cleaner on the contents of all international calls, recording every single one, so long as it was not targeting a specific person in the US.

The NSA resents the use of the phrase "vacuum cleaner." It argues that it doesn't want to vacuum up all international calls and couldn't process them even if it did. We use "vacuum cleaner" because the bill would permit without a warrant the untargeted collection of many, many calls, without the particularized suspicion required by the Constitution for government searches.

FISA's "Radio Exception" Should Be Repealed

As partial justification for the warrantless interception of all international calls, the Administration's section-by-section analysis and its earlier discussions of this issue refer to FISA's distinction between wire and radio communications, without actually explaining it or justifying why an exception for radio portions of communications should be extended to all communications. We will explain here that the "radio exception" was meant to be temporary, that it is now clearly outdated and that it should be abolished.

When FISA was adopted, it exempted international telephone calls (and other communications) entering and leaving the US by satellite. The Administration unquestioningly accepts this exemption for the radio portion of communications and argues that it should be applied to communications carried by wire, thus exempting from privacy protection all international communications of Americans.

It is clear from FISA's legislative history that Congress intended to consider subsequent legislation to regulate interception of radio communications. . . .

The "radio exception" may have been justified in 1978 on the ground that the government was worried about disclosing to carriers the subjects of its interest, or that the carriers were reluctant to cooperate with surveillance, or that the carriers may not have had the ability to isolate the communications of a targeted person or communications instrument. None of those reasons appears valid today. It is clear that carriers are willing and able to cooperate; and the Communications Assistance for Law Enforcement Act of 1994 requires all carriers to build into their networks the ability to isolate the communications to and from specific users. . . .

The privacy intrusion and the likely harm are the same regardless of whether a person's communications are intercepted because the government was intentionally targeting him or because the government was scanning millions of calls.

Whatever was the purpose of the radio exception in 1978, there is no reason to apply different standards today. But rather than reconciling the standards by providing satellite communications the same protections that have always applied to wire communications, the Administration would respond by rolling back the protections afforded wire communications and exempting all international communications from FISA, unless the government is targeting a known person in the US. A much better way to make the statute technology neutral is to require a warrant for all interception of communications with one leg in the US.

FISA's Dichotomy Between Targeted vs. Non-Targeted Surveillance Should Be Eliminated

The Administration's bill, without explanation, perpetuates a distinction drawn in 1978 between the targeted and untargeted interception of communications. In 1978, FISA required a warrant for the acquisition of a radio communication to or from the US only if the contents were acquired by "intentionally targeting" a particular, known US person who is in the US. The Administration would extend this rule to wire communications as well, thus allowing the untargeted acquisition of the communications of a US person.

The question Congress should ask is: What difference does it make to an American that the government collected, analyzed and disseminated his communications without suspecting him of any involvement in terrorism or espionage versus specifically targeting him? The privacy intrusion and the likely harm are the same regardless of whether a person's communications are intercepted because the government was intentionally targeting him or because the government was scanning millions of calls and his were selected as suspicious based on some criteria other than his name. In either case, suspicion may fall on an American and he may face adverse consequences. And in either case, the key question should be how reliable were the selection criteria.

The origins of the distinction between targeting and non-targeting may go back to an issue of major concern at the time FISA was enacted, namely, the "watch-listing" of Americans for NSA surveillance. In the 1960s and 1970s, a practice grew up of watch-listing Americans who were politically active in opposing the Vietnam War or advocating other political positions at odds with the Administration or the views of the leadership of the FBI. One of the purposes of FISA was to prevent the watch-listing of Americans without a court order.

Today, while there are concerns that the Administration has been investigating and harassing political activists, a new concern has emerged: that the data mining and profiling activities of various agencies are causing people real harm in their daily lives. In these cases, the government is not intentionally targeting a particular, known US person. Instead, the government is casting a broad net, using computers to apply selection criteria to oceans of data and selecting out suspicion individuals.

The fact that the selection does not start with a known person does not make the process any less consequential for the privacy of the person whose communications are ultimately selected for scrutiny.

Limiting the definition of "electronic surveillance" to the intentional targeting of a particular, known person seems especially unjustified given the fact that today most selection of communications is computerized, either by the service provider at the direction of the government or by the government itself. Sometimes selection is done by name, sometimes by telephone number or email address or IP address number, and sometimes based on another set of parameters. In all cases, the government should have a solid reason to believe that its criteria will isolate communications that are to or from a foreign power or an agent of a foreign power and that will contain foreign intelligence. In all cases, whether the government uses a name, a telephone number, or a complex set of screens, the process of defining those selection criteria should be subject to judicial scrutiny, based on a finding of probable cause to believe that the communications to be processed will be those of an agent of a foreign power and will contain foreign intelligence.

The current rule and the Administration's bill make no sense, requiring a court order when the government is selecting for interception the communications of a particular, known person but not requiring a court order when the government is selecting communications based on some other criteria. The solution, it seems, is to require a court order for all processing intended to select communications for presentation to a human being. Whether that is a name or a number or a complicated set of screens, the government is selecting for scrutiny the private communications of individuals in circumstances in which those individuals may face adverse consequences, and in our society that is precisely the type of question that should be submitted to prior judicial approval.

CHAPTER 4

How Are New Technologies Affecting Domestic Wiretapping?

Chapter Preface

Many people think of wiretapping as listening in on calls made to or from a wired phone. The dictionary defines "wiretap" as "to tap a telephone or telegraph wire in order to get information," and in the past, that was all it meant. But today, people have other ways of communicating, and many do not use wired phones at all—they use cordless phones, cell phones, and the Internet. Even voice messages on wired phones do not travel by wire all the way between the two parties, as they once did, but are transmitted via satellites or fiber-optic cables. In addition, text messages are sent over the Internet. Furthermore, investigators get information not only from the *content* of a suspect's communications, but from the *transaction data* about incoming and outgoing calls over a period of time, about e-mail, and about electronic credit card transactions. All these forms of electronic surveillance are now informally referred to as wiretapping.

Investigators do not actually eavesdrop on most of the calls that interest them. First, there are far too many communications for more than a small fraction to be listened to or examined, and second, monitoring content requires more legal authorization than does analyzing transaction data. The latter process is extremely complex and can reveal a great deal of personal information about the subject of an investigation—so much that more and more people are becoming concerned about the invasion of privacy it involves. The National Security Agency (NSA) collects vast amounts of transaction data, and new ways of interpreting it are being developed, but the details of this process are classified (secret). Although the government has assured Americans that the NSA is not listening to the content of their phone calls, that does not mean nothing is being learned about the private lives of law-abiding citizens.

In 1994 the Communications Assistance for Law Enforcement Act (CALEA) was passed, requiring all communication services to provide means for law enforcement officials to access communications secretly. This requirement complicates development of new technologies, especially in the case of voice calls transmitted over the Internet. On the whole, however, advances in technology have complicated surveillance, rather than the other way around. Many experts worry because in the attempt to discover criminals and terrorists through screening of communication transaction data, investigators unintentionally include innocent people, simply because the software used to process the data is inclusive rather than selective.

Much of the controversy about wiretapping is the result of technological change. It is against the law to wiretap domestic communications without a search warrant, but it has become hard to define just what "domestic" means because many foreign communications are now physically routed through switching points in the United States. Because it is more practical than physically tapping fiber-optic cables underneath the ocean, the NSA accesses foreign calls from the U.S. switching points. At first this was done through a program that many considered illegal; as of 2008 the program is legal—yet it is still controversial, because ordinary Americans make international calls (which was not common in the past), and they have a right to privacy. However, many people believe it is essential to monitor the communications of terrorists and potential terrorists. So no solution had been found as of 2008.

In 2008, Congress had begun new hearings about wiretapping laws. To understand the debate being reported in the news, it is necessary to know something about the technological issues involved.

The Communications Assistance for Law Enforcement Act (CALEA) Modernizes Wiretapping

Leslie Ellis

Leslie Ellis is an independent technology analyst and writer.

Among the dozen or so external links on the to-do list for launching carrier-grade telephone service is a nine-year-old law, known as the Communications Assistance for Law Enforcement Act, or CALEA.

In general, CALEA is to modern, digital telephony, what wiretapping is to traditional analog telephony. It usually enters the life of the cable technologist on a piece of paper with the words "court order" written on it. The court order is in the clutches of a uniformed police officer, who is standing in the lobby, and who needs immediate access to the call records of a suspected criminal. In some cases, the order also requires a way to anonymously duplicate calls made by, or received from, that suspect.

The reasons for CALEA are palpable: The bottomless appetite among people to talk to each other isn't confined to the blameless. Bad guys talk to each other, too. Add in the flourish of new communication methods, and the woes of the law enforcement community intensify.

Electronic surveillance can be a wild goose chase for police and FBI officers.

The available methods for the bad guys to talk to each other are plentiful—and increasing. Since court-ordered wiretapping began, in 1970, cellular and satellite signal paths emerged. So did call digitization, packetization and the use of the Internet as a signal path.

These days, a call from one place to another can move over any of four networks beyond the traditional Public Switched Telephone Network (PSTN). As a direct result, electronic surveillance can be a wild goose chase for police and FBI officers.

In practice, drugs are the catalyst for most telecommunication intercepts. Of 1,491 court orders issued to authorize electronic surveillance in 2001, 78 percent (1,167) targeted narcotics offenders, according to the Administrative Office of the United States Courts. A far second: Gambling offenses (82).

And, of those nearly 1,500 intercepts, most were invoked on cellular telephone users. Of those cable providers who offer residential telephone service, all say that they're ready for CALEA. Some, like Cox Communications, have assisted law enforcement officials with their electronic surveillance needs from time to time—but they say that the number of wiretaps requested remains pretty small. CALEA, they say, is the kind of thing that needs an action plan more than it needs constant attention—like fire drills.

CALEA requires that law enforcement officers get what they need, without tipping off the suspect.

What Law Enforcement Needs

What usually matters most to police and FBI officials, when it comes to electronic surveillance, is immediacy. When the uniformed police officer shows up in the lobby with the court order, he or she doesn't want to hear that it'll take three or so days to get the CALEA gear up, any more than the firefighter ants to hear that it'll take three days to get a bucket of water. Throughout the law itself, CALEA makes frequent use of the word "expeditiously."

And, CALEA cares little about underlying technologies. Law enforcement officials need two things: Call details, and call content. Call details are everything a phone can do—dial numbers, receive dialed numbers, forward calls, initiate or participate in three-way calls, and any of the rest of the SS7 features. Call content, in the analog world, is a wiretap. In digital telephony, call content means setting up a duplicate packet stream, which can be routed to multiple police or FBI officers.

Lastly, CALEA requires that law enforcement officers get what they need, without tipping off the suspect. Just like in the movies, when a click on the line scared off a phone conversation of nefarious intent, today's digital, packet networks can't introduce any latencies or problems that would scare off today's high-tech criminal.

The FBI, and behind it, the U.S. Attorney General, shepherds CALEA implementations. In most cases, the FBI provides CALEA software modules; when the law was introduced, $500 million was set aside to reimburse both carriers and switch manufacturers for CALEA-related expenses. (Don't get too excited. The law is nine years old; most of the CALEA disbursements have already been made.)

In its documentation about CALEA, the FBI openly favors "flexible deployment," described as "the deployment of CALEA-compliant solutions in accordance with normal generic upgrade cycles—where such deployment will not delay implementation of CALEA solutions in areas of high priority to law enforcement officials." In other words, do it when you launch phone, but don't make them wait.

New providers of residential phone service, such as cable operators, can also file a "Safe Harbor" document with the FCC, which indicates the methods by which they plan to implement CALEA. According to Section 107(a)(2) of CALEA, "a telecommunications carrier shall be found to be in compliance ... if the carrier is in compliance with publicly available technical requirements or standards adopted by an industry association or standard-setting organization, or by the FCC."

To that end, both PacketCable, and ANSI/SCTE Standard 24-13, describe a functional representation of how CALEA can be implemented in cable phone environments. Traditional telcos use a standard, developed by subcommittee TR-45.2 of the Telecommunications Industry Association, known as J-STD-025. It specifies the necessary interfaces for delivering intercepted communications and call-identifying information to law enforcement agencies.

Circuit-Switched vs. VoIP

In the old days of analog telephone, two devices—the "pen register" and the "trap and trace" device—were used to help police in surveillance. Both devices are still widely used in surveillance discussions.

The term "pen register" dates back to the days of telegraphs, and describes a machine that uses ink and ticker tape to record and display telegraph pulses. Today, the "pen register" essentially references the ability to interpret outgoing information.

These days, new techniques are used to conduct electronic surveillance. Predictably, implementing CALEA differs, depending on whether a cable phone provider is using circuit switched/constant bit rate or packetized, IP-based gear.

In a circuit-switched scenario, a specifically-entrusted cable system employee provisions the switch for surveillance on a particular target. "Specifically-entrusted" usually means the person who handles security and piracy protection, or, in the case of CALEA, the person who can work quickly, intelligently, and quietly.

That person provisions the Class-5 switch so that relevant data can be diverted to an outgoing port, for collection by the FBI. Capturing call content is accomplished through a conference bridge, where one leg of the call is anonymously linked to the law.

Gathering call detail and content in a packet-based, IP environment isn't quite as straightforward. A voice call made over the public Internet uses the methods of the Internet, which break a bunch of packets into clumps, and send them over varying routes to their destination. The route itself can change from one call to the next.

The industry's PacketCable specifications include methods for dealing with CALEA. PacketCable breaks CALEA-oriented activities into functional requirements, which can be variously interpreted by suppliers. Still, though, because PacketCable essentially duplicates the PSTN in software, implementing CALEA is tricky.

One cable provider active with VoIP [Voice over Internet Protocol] cites call forwarding as the trickiest task for CALEA. Consider the intercept target, active on a cable VoIP system, who forwards all incoming calls to a cell phone. In the parlance of PacketCable, it is not enough to depend on the CMTS (cable modem termination system) to capture call content.

In that scenario, the call comes in from the PSTN, to a media gateway. A call management server, provisioned for CALEA, recognizes the call as an intercept target. But, since the suspect is forwarding all calls, usually to a cell phone, the call may not ever leave the gateway. In short, relying only on a three-way bridge, or a CMTS capture, may not work—the media gateway also needs to be involved.

All vendors of VoIP equipment for cable are aware of CALEA, and offer modules or stand-alone servers to address the need for electronic surveillance. But, because VoIP in cable is still relatively new, it's fair to say that its CALEA efforts have yet to settle into a pattern.

Some suppliers, for example, combine CALEA directly into a softswitch. Others isolate CALEA into a separate server. PacketCable allows for integrated or standalone handling.

Catching the Bad Guys

Cable operators getting ready for phone, whether circuit-switched or VoIP, are aware of CALEA, and are setting up methods to comply. Mostly, notes one cable MSO technologist, getting ready for CALEA means figuring out different possible scenarios, especially given the many features and routes offered by broadband, IP communication networks. Call flows can get pretty complicated, pretty fast.

But, despite the complexity, electronic surveillance appears to work. The 1,491 court-ordered wiretaps in 2001 produced 3,683 arrests, and 732 convictions—proof enough that electronic surveillance is a valuable tool in catching the bad guys.

Wiretapping Could Stifle Internet Phone Technology

Dean Takahashi

Dean Takahashi is a columnist for the San Jose Mercury News.

In its zeal to pursue terrorists and criminals, the federal government could crush a nascent technology and, ironically, jeopardize the nation's security. That's one of the consequences of enabling wiretapping in the digital age.

At the request of the FBI, the Federal Communications Commission is soon expected to require companies that provide certain kinds of Internet phone calls to enable law enforcement to conduct wiretapping, given court approval.

Conventional phone calls are already subject to wiretapping when law enforcement obtains a court order.

Internet phone calls, also called VOIP for voice over Internet protocol, can bypass phone-system charges by using the Internet to route calls from one Internet user to another. That makes for cheap or free calls—but complicates wiretapping.

Some Internet companies loop calls through the existing phone system, making it possible to wiretap them at that junction. The FCC has set a That's OK for companies such as Vonage, which allows computers to connect to the traditional telephone system and have a centralized architecture compatible with wiretapping methods. A spokeswoman for Vonage confirms it can comply with the FCC regulation.

But companies that link calls from one Internet user to another, bypassing the phone system, are exempt.

EBay's Skype, which uses a combination of a centralized and a more flexible user-to-user architecture known as peer-to-peer, may or may not be able to comply, particularly when callers are on the move. Skype declined to comment.

Dean Takahashi, "Wiretapping Could Stifle VOIP Technology," *San Jose Mercury News*, February 6, 2007. www.mercurynews.com. Reproduced by permission.

Its SkypeIn and SkypeOut services allow users to make or receive calls on the traditional telephone system with a Skype Internet phone. Those calls are probably subject to the wiretapping requirements. Presumably, Skype would simply refer the FBI to the phone company in question.

But it appears from its legal maneuvers that the FBI may also want to find a way to tap peer-to-peer calls, the ones that bypass the telephone system. And the FCC's analysis of the FBI request suggests it might go along with a move to require wiretapping on any new Internet communications system.

That's something the technology lobby adamantly opposes, says John Morris, director of Internet standards at the Center for Democracy and Technology in Washington.

For one, Morris says, that would totally stretch the 1994 law the FBI has used to extend wiretapping to Internet calls: The Communications Assistance for Law Enforcement Act requires phone companies to allow wiretapping if it's technically possible on their networks. In 2004, the FBI moved to extend the law to Internet calls, and in 2005, the FCC agreed. The CDT and other groups challenged the ruling, but an appeals court sided with the FBI and FCC in June 2006.

If we hobble technology to help law enforcement, we make ourselves vulnerable, not safer.

As the deadline for extending wiretapping to Internet calls approaches, Morris doesn't know what companies such as Skype will do. Time will tell as the FBI comes to the company with requests to tap calls.

A call made on a laptop using Skype software may be hard to find, let alone wiretap.

Complying with the Law Would Hobble Technology

To comply with the wiretapping rule, a service such as Skype might have to centralize its architecture and forgo communications innovations the current architecture offers. Or eBay might sell Skype to an offshore entity. Or Skype could deign a backdoor, or vulnerability, into the technology to enable wiretapping.

That not only would be ridiculous, but hobbling a communications network in such a way would also expose it to criminals with the technical know-how to exploit it.

"It's bad policy to cut off the benefits of VOIP and make it vulnerable," agrees Whit Diffie, chief security officer at Sun Microsystems.

The FBI and FCC declined interview requests. In a 2005 court filing, the Department of Justice said it was in the interest of public safety and national security to extend wiretapping to Internet calls and that any exceptions should be rare. Kevin Martin, chairman of the FCC, said in a statement at the time that it would give law enforcement the tools to keep up with rapid technological change.

But Diffie and Sun colleague Susan Landau wrote a white paper expressing their concerns in June 2006. They were joined by representatives of Intel, telecommunications company NeuStar, Applied Signal Technology, and several academics, including a former National Security Agency member.

The FCC hasn't yet required Skype to build an infrastructure that would allow Internet calls that bypass the phone system to be tapped. Diffie guesses such an infrastructure could ruin the flexibility of the current architecture and cost billions of dollars.

Morris remains concerned that the FBI wants to bring these peer-to-peer calls into wiretapping compliance—or make them illegal.

We are not at that point yet. But Landau warns this kind of regulation is a slippery slope. If peer-to-peer calls become illegal in the United States, the technology will move offshore. Other nations will innovate, and we won't compete as well.

We have to balance the need to enforce laws with the need to move technology forward and at the same time protect our privacy. If we hobble technology to help law enforcement, we make ourselves vulnerable, not safer.

We faced this kind of issue in the early 1990s, when the debate was about whether to allow encryption technologies strong enough to hide data from the government. The government later decided to allow strong encryption to be used unencumbered, particularly as the technology was allowed overseas. The outcome here may be the same.

Can the Government Track Cell Phones Without Showing Probable Cause?

Scott Cameron

Scott Cameron is an attorney in a California law firm.

Here's the next step Big Brother is taking toward an Orwellian 1984: Your cellular telephone can pinpoint your location any time it's turned on. That's right. Any time your cell phone is turned on and within range of a cellular tower, it is communicating with that tower to broadcast your location. It has to. Otherwise you couldn't get your incoming calls. Federal law enforcement agencies have figured this out, and if you are someone a federal law enforcement agency is looking for, they are using that to track you.

Here's how it works: These days, everyone has a cell phone. Since the end of 2005, the Federal Communications Commission has mandated that cell phone service providers must be able to locate 67% of all callers to within 100 meters, and 95% of all callers within 300 meters. Cell phone companies have a variety of ways of doing this. They can triangulate your position by using three cell towers to fix your position. Others have gone one step further, and most new cell phones come with a GPS chip which can be used to pinpoint your position to within a few feet. The cell phone companies record your location data as determined either through triangulation or from the GPS chip, and store it as "historical location" information. An important feature in this equation, however, is the ability of your cell phone service carrier to transmit "real-time" location information (of your cell phone, anyway) to law enforcement at any time. And since "everyone" carries

Scott Cameron, "Your Cell Phone Is a Homing Beacon—Should the Government Be Allowed to Use It Without Showing Probable Cause?" *IP Law Blog*, April 12, 2006. www.theiplawblog.com. Reproduced by permission.

their cell phone, the government has a pretty good chance of tracking you down if they need to. Big Brother is watching.

Now this is not necessarily a bad thing. If you are someone wanted by the FBI or another federal law enforcement agency, maybe the FBI should be able to get information from your cell phone company that would pinpoint your location. In fact, no one is seriously saying that the FBI cannot get access to that information. The real question is rather what showing is required for the government to gain such access. As to historical location information, the Stored Communications Act, provides that the government need only demonstrate "articulable facts as to why such records are relevant to an ongoing investigation." This is a significantly lower showing than the government must make to get a search warrant. For that, it must demonstrate "probable cause that the information sought will lead to evidence of a crime." The government is asserting that they need only satisfy this same rather lax "articulable facts" standard for getting real-time location information rather than showing probable cause that the information will yield evidence of a crime. The question of required showing by the government has been causing quite a stir in the federal courts recently.

Court Decisions

The first court to publish a decision regarding the government's required showing was the Southern District of New York. On August 25, 2005, Magistrate Judge James Orenstein denied the government's request for real-time cell site location information. The court had previously granted the government's request for installation and use of a pen register and trap and trace device, which allowed the government to obtain the numbers which call the phone or are called by it, and the time those calls are made. The pen register and tap and trace device are clearly available by federal statutes. But the importance of this decision is that Judge Orenstein denied the site location information that would provide real-time location because the government failed to provide information establishing the probable cause that would be required for a warrant. The judge noted that he had granted similar requests in the past, and quoted Justice Frankfurter: "Wisdom too often never comes, and so one ought not reject it merely because it comes late."

As technology continues to advance, law enforcement naturally looks to find ways to use that technology to improve its efficiency.

Following Judge Orenstein's stand, several magistrate judges have been confronted with similar requests for location information derived from cell phone tracking. In fact, a dozen decisions have issued regarding the requested cell site information since that decision. The requests at issue, like the request Judge Orenstain confronted, were not accompanied by affidavits establishing probable cause that evidence of a crime would be discovered. Instead, the government stated that the information would be relevant to an ongoing investigation, thus apparently satisfying the less stringent standard required to get the historical location information. All but two of these decisions have denied the government's request.

On December 20, 2005, Magistrate Judge Gabriel W. Gorenstein, of the Southern District of New York, became the first to agree with the government's arguments in a published opinion. While it is a complex issue, the court reasoned that the cell location information sought was covered by the Pen Register Statute, which would provide authority for the order if not for a provision of . . . the Communications Assistance for Law Enforcement Act of 1994, [which] provides that information acquired solely pursuant to the authority of pen registers and trap and trace devices shall not include any information that may disclose the physical location of the cell phone customer. Judge Gorenstein found that the information sought was not acquired solely pursuant to the authority of pen registers and trap and trace devices.

Almost every other published case has disagreed with Judge Gorenstein. Only Magistrate Judge Hornsby in Louisiana has agreed with Judge Gorenstein. (A magistrate judge in West Virginia granted the government's request. It did so, however, after rejecting the government's arguments about statutory authority for the cell location information and holding instead that the individual in question had no expectation of privacy in the cell phone because the phone in question did not belong to him. It belonged to a friend.)

No Government Review of Cases

Almost all of these cases have another similarity. In each case, the magistrate judge issuing the opinion denying the government's request has invited the government to seek review of the denial so that the magistrate judges will have guidance as they continue to encounter this issue. The government has not yet seen fit to seek review of any of these cases. As the government appears ex parte in each case, and the individual never even knows he is being tracked, there is no one else to seek review. Thus, the government seems willing, and able, to deprive the courts of any higher level guidance of the required showing it must make to receive the cell location information it seeks.

As technology continues to advance, law enforcement naturally looks to find ways to use that technology to improve its efficiency. The concern must be drawing the proper fine between efficiency of law enforcement and protecting the privacy of the citizens. It is up to the courts to recognize, as Judge Orenstein did in this case, when that line is approached, and when it is crossed. And when magistrate judges across the country invite the government to seek review of their decisions to provide guidance from higher courts and the government declines all such requests, instead remaining content with the rulings against them, it begins to raise suspicions. If this is a valuable tool for law enforcement to use to protect citizens more efficiently and effectively, and clearly it is, why does the government resist all efforts to establish the limits of the use of that tool? Big Brother?

The NSA Is Using Unperfected Technology in Domestic Surveillance

Shane Harris

Shane Harris is the Intelligence and Homeland Security correspondent for National Journal. *He also writes for other national publications.*

The Bush administration has assiduously avoided any talk about the actual workings of its program to intercept the phone calls and e-mails of people in the United States who are suspected of having links to terrorists abroad. Officials' unwavering script goes like this: Present the legal justifications for the president to authorize domestic electronic surveillance without warrants, but say nothing about how the National Security Agency actually does it—or about what else the agency might be doing.

But when Attorney General Alberto Gonzales appeared before the Senate Judiciary Committee on February 6 [2006] to answer questions about the program, what he didn't say pulled back the curtain on how the NSA decides which calls and e-mails to monitor. The agency bases those decisions on a broad and less focused surveillance than officials have publicly described, a surveillance that may, or may not, be legal. . . .

On February 28, Gonzales sent committee Chairman Arlen Specter, R-Pa., a six-page letter, partly to respond to questions he was unprepared to answer at the hearing, but also "to clarify certain of my responses" in the earlier testimony. . . . With exacting language, he narrowed the scope of his comments to address only "questions relating to the specific NSA activities that have been publicly confirmed by the president." Then, as if to avoid any confusion, Gonzales added, "Those activities involve the interception by the NSA of the contents of communications" involving suspected terrorists and people in the United States.

Considering that terrorists often talk and write in code, the transactional data of a communication . . . could yield more valuable intelligence than the content.

Slightly, and with a single word, Gonzales was tipping his hand. The content of electronic communications is usually considered to be the spoken words of a phone call or the written words in an electronic message. The term does not include the wealth of so-called transactional data that accompany every communication: a phone number, and what calls were placed to and from that number; the time a call was placed; whether the call was answered and how long it lasted, down to the second; the time and date that an e-mail message was sent, as well as its unique address and routing path, which reveals the location of the computer that sent it and, presumably, the author.

Considering that terrorists often talk and write in code, the transactional data of a communication, properly exploited, could yield more valuable intelligence than the content itself. "You will get a very full picture of a person's associations and their patterns of activity," said Jim Dempsey, the policy director of the Center for Democracy and Technology, an electronic-privacy advocacy group. "You'll know who they're talking to, when they're talking, how long, how frequently. . . . It's a lot [of information]. I mean, a lot."

According to sources who are familiar with the details of what the White House calls the "terrorist surveillance program," and who asked to remain anonymous because the program is still classified, analyzing transactional data is one of the first and most important steps the agency takes in deciding which phone calls to listen to and which electronic messages to read. Far from the limited or targeted surveillance that Gonzales, President Bush, and intelligence officials have described, this traffic analysis examines thousands, perhaps hundreds of thousands, of individuals, because nearly every phone number and nearly every e-mail address is connected to a person.

Patterns in the Sea

Analysis of telephone traffic patterns helps analysts and investigators spot relationships among people that aren't always obvious. For instance, imagine that a man in Portland, Ore., receives a call from someone at a pay phone in Brooklyn, N.Y., every Tuesday at 9 a.m. Also every Tuesday, but minutes earlier, the pay phone caller rings up a man in Miami. An investigator might look at that pattern and suspect that the men in Portland and Miami are communicating through the Brooklyn caller, who's acting as a kind of courier, to mask their relationship. Patterns like this have led criminal investigators into the inner workings of drug cartels and have proved vital in breaking these cartels up.

Terrorists employ similar masking techniques. They use go-betweens to circuitously route calls, and they change cellphones often to avoid detection. Transactional data, however, capture these behaviors. If NSA analysts—or their computers—can find these patterns or signatures, then they might find the terrorists, or at least know which ones they should monitor.

Just after 9/11, according to knowledgeable sources, the NSA began intercepting the communications of specific foreign persons and groups named on a list. The sources didn't specify whether persons inside the United States were monitored as part of that list. But a former government official who is knowledgeable about NSA activities and the warrantless surveillance program said that this original list of people and groups, or others like it, could have formed the base of the NSA's surveillance of transactional data, the parts of a communication that aren't considered content.

If the agency started with a list of phone numbers, it could find all the numbers dialed from those phones. The NSA could then learn what numbers were called from that second list of numbers, and what calls that list received, and so on, "pushing out" the lists until the agency had identified a vast network of callers and their transactional data, the former official said. The agency might eavesdrop on only a few conversations or e-mails. But starting with even an initial target list of, say, 10 phone numbers quickly yields a web of hundreds of thousands of communications, because the volume increases exponentially with every new layer of callers.

Not long after the surveillance program started, in October 2001, the NSA began looking for new tools to mine the telecom data.

To find meaningful patterns in transactional data, analysts need a lot of it. They must set baselines about what constitutes "normal" behavior versus "suspicious" activity. Administration officials have said that the NSA doesn't intercept the contents of a communication unless officials have a "reasonable" basis to conclude that at least one party is linked to a terrorist organization. To make any reasonable determination like that, the agency needs hundreds of thousands, or even millions, of call records, preferably as soon as they are created, said a senior person in the defense industry who is familiar with the NSA program and is an expert in the analytical tools used to find patterns and connections. Asked if this means that the NSA program is much broader and less targeted than administration officials have described, the expert replied, "I think that's correct."

In theory, finding reasonable connections in data is a straightforward and largely automated process. Analysts use computer programs based on algorithms—mathematical procedures for solving a particular problem—much the same way that meteorologists use data models to forecast the weather. Counter-terrorism algorithms look for the transactional indicators that match what analysts recognize as signs of a plot.

Predicting Terrorism

Of course, those algorithms must be sophisticated enough to spot many not-so-obvious patterns in a mass of data that are mostly uninteresting, and they work best when the data come from many sources. Algorithms have proven useful for detecting frequent criminal activity, such as credit card fraud. "Historical data clearly indicate that if a credit card turns up in two cities on two continents on the same day, that's a useful pattern," says Jeff Jonas, a computer scientist who invented a technology to connect known scam artists who are on casinos' watch lists with new potential grifters, and is now the chief scientist of IBM Entity Analytics. "The challenge of predicting terrorism is that unlike fraud, we don't have the same volume of historical data to learn from," Jonas said. "Compounding this is the fact that terrorists are constantly changing their methods and do their best to avoid leaving any digital footprints in the first place."

The obvious solution would be to write an algorithm that is flexible and fast enough to weigh millions of pieces of evidence, including exculpatory ones, against each other. But according to technology experts, and even the NSA's own stated research accomplishments, that technology has not been perfected.

The NSA began soon after the 9/11 terrorist attacks to collect transactional data from telecommunications companies. Several telecom executives said in press accounts that their companies gave the NSA access to their switches, the terminals that handle most of the country's electronic traffic. One executive told *National Journal* that NSA officials urged him to hand over his company's call logs. When he resisted, the officials implied that most of his competitors had acceded to the agency's request.

Not long after the surveillance program started, in October 2001, the NSA began looking for new tools to mine the telecom data. The agency, the industry expert said, considered some that the Defense Department's Total Information Awareness program was developing. TIA was an ambitious and controversial experiment to find patterns of terrorist activity in a much broader range of transactions than just telephone data. But NSA officials rejected the TIA tools because they were "too brittle," the expert said, meaning that they failed to manage the torrent of data that the NSA wanted to analyze. He noted the irony of rejecting the TIA technologies—which privacy advocates had characterized as huge, all-seeing, digital dragnets—because they couldn't handle the size of the NSA's load.

If analysts are working with algorithms designed to detect only certain patterns, they could be missing others.

In the fall of 2002, a federal research-and-development agency that builds technologies primarily for the NSA launched another search for pattern-detection solutions. The Advanced Research and Development Activity, ARDA, issued $64 million in contracts for the Novel Intelligence for Massive Data, or NIMD, program. Its goal was "to help analysts deal with information overload, detect early indicators of strategic surprise, and avoid analytic errors," according to ARDA's public call for proposals released last year. In essence, NIMD is an early-warning system, which is how the administration has described the terrorist surveillance program. In 2003, ARDA also took over research of the tools being developed under TIA.

Less-Sophisticated Tools

While the NSA was searching for the next generation of data-sifters, it continued to rely on less sophisticated tools. For an example, the former government official who spoke to *NJ* cited applications that organize data into broad categories, allowing analysts to see some relationships but obscuring some of the nuance in the underlying information. The results of this kind of category analysis can be displayed on a graph. But the graph might reveal only how many times a particular word appears in a conversation, not necessarily the significance of the word or how it relates to other words. Technologists sarcastically call these diagrams BAGs—big-ass graphs.

Such was the state of affairs when the NSA started looking for terrorist patterns in a telephonic ocean. So, instead of looking for a tool that could cull through the data, the agency decided to "reverse" the process, starting with the data set and working backward, looking for algorithms that could work with it.

The NSA has made some breakthroughs, the industry expert said, but its solution relies in part on a technological "trick," which he wouldn't disclose. Another data-mining expert, who also asked not to be identified because the NSA's work is classified, said that computer engineers probably started with the telecom companies' call data, looked for patterns, and then wrote algorithms to detect them as they went along, tweaking the algorithms as needed.

Such an ad hoc approach is brittle in its own right. For starters, if analysts are working with algorithms designed to detect only certain patterns, they could be missing others, the technology expert said. At the same time, the more dependent the algorithms are on identifying very specific patterns of behavior, the more vulnerable the NSA's monitoring is to being foiled if terrorists discover what the agency is watching for, or if they change their behavior. A more complex algorithm that considers thousands, or even millions, of patterns is harder to defeat.

In an unsophisticated system, connections among people can emerge that look suspicious but are actually meaningless.

The industry expert added that NSA officials have worried that "if you knew what the technical trick was they were doing [to make the surveillance program function], you wouldn't have to know what specific algorithms" the agency was using. This reliance on a "trick" makes the program very vulnerable to defeat and helps explain why the Bush administration is so keen on cloaking its inner workings.

"It's pretty bleeding-edge," the expert said, referring to a technology that's unperfected and therefore prone to instability. "We're talking about dumping hundreds of thousands or millions of records" into a system. In an unsophisticated system, connections among people can emerge that look suspicious but are actually meaningless. A book agent who represents a journalist who once interviewed Osama bin Laden, for example, doesn't herself necessarily know bin Laden. But she might turn up in an NSA search of transactional data. "False positives will happen," the expert said.

Gonzales and former NSA Director Michael V. Hayden have said that career agency employees decide to eavesdrop only if they have a "reasonable" basis to believe one party to a communication is a terrorist or connected to a terrorist organization. But what determines reasonableness?...

If the technology the NSA is using to determine what constitutes a reasonable search is unsophisticated, the industry expert said, "you're talking about tapping a phone based on a statistical correlation."...

New Legal Questions

As more about the NSA's operations become known, new legal questions arise, including one that goes to the heart of how officials reasonably identify suspected terrorists.

Under normal criminal law, content is defined as "any information concerning the substance, purport, or meaning of [a] communication," but the definition of content under the law that governs electronic eavesdropping on U.S. persons for intelligence purposes is different and is potentially in conflict with normal jurisprudence. That law, the Foreign Intelligence Surveillance Act, states that content "includes any information concerning the identity of the parties . . . or the existence, substance, purport, or meaning of [their] communication."

A phone number can be used to identify a person, said Dempsey of the Center for Democracy and Technology, who for nine years was assistant counsel to the House Judiciary Subcommittee on Civil and Constitutional Rights. Does that mean that a phone number is "content" under the law? FISA, enacted in 1978, didn't envision today's technology, when anyone with an Internet connection can use a phone number to find someone's name, address, and even an aerial photograph of his house, Dempsey said.

"I just cannot read [FISA] and figure out what it means in the context of analysis of [transactional] data," he added. "Presumably somebody in the administration thinks they understand it. . . . Whether that's providing any clear guidance" to the people working on the NSA program, "that's not clear."

Organizations to Contact

The editors have compiled the following list of organizations concerned with the issues debated in this book. The descriptions are derived from materials provided by the organizations. All have publications or information available for interested readers. The list was compiled on the date of publication of the present volume; the information provided here may change. Readers need to remember that many organizations take several weeks or longer to respond to inquiries.

American Civil Liberties Union (ACLU)
125 Broad St., 18th Floor, New York, NY 10004
212-549-2585
Web site: www.aclu.org

The ACLU is a nonprofit, nongovernmental organization that works to preserve constitutional protections and guarantees: First Amendment rights, the right to equal protection under the law, the right to due process, and the right to privacy, that is, freedom from unwarranted government intrusion into personal and private affairs. It is involved in political activism and supports lawsuits on behalf of people whose rights are threatened. Its large Web site has sections with material covering various issues, including one titled "Safe and Free," which deals with domestic surveillance.

Center for American Progress (CAP)
1333 H St. NW, 10th Floor, Washington, DC 20005
202-682-1611
e-mail: progress@americanprogress.org
Web site: www.americanprogress.org

The Center for American Progress is a progressive think tank dedicated to improving the lives of Americans through ideas and action. The CAP Web site contains many articles by experts in different areas of public policy, for example, "A Legal Analysis of the NSA Warrantless Surveillance Program" by Morton H. Halperin. CAP publishes newsletters on a variety of topics.

Center for Constitutional Rights (CCR)
666 Broadway, 7th Floor, New York, NY   10012
212-614-6464
Web site: http://ccrjustice.org

The Center for Constitutional Rights is dedicated to advancing and protecting the rights guaranteed by the U.S. Constitution and the Universal Declaration of Human Rights. The CCR is a nonprofit legal and educational organization committed to the creative use of law as a positive force for social change. Its Web site has a section on surveillance that includes a podcast about the NSA warrantless wiretapping program.

Center for Democracy and Technology (CDT)
1634 Eye St. NW, Suite 1100, Washington, DC   20006
202-637-9800 • fax: 202-637-0968
Web site: www.cdt.org

The Center for Democracy and Technology works to promote democratic values and constitutional liberties in the digital age. With expertise in law, technology, and policy, the CDT seeks practical ways to enhance free expression and privacy in global communications technologies and is dedicated to building consensus among all parties interested in the future of the Internet and other new communications media. Its Web site contains articles, testimonies, and speeches that deal with various forms of domestic surveillance.

Center for National Security Studies (CNSS)
1120 Nineteenth St. NW, 8th Floor, Washington, DC   20036
202-721-5650 • fax: 202-530-0128
e-mail: cnss@cnss.org
Web site: www.cnss.org

The Center for National Security Studies, a nongovernmental advocacy and research organization, was founded in 1974 to work for control of the FBI and CIA and to prevent violations of civil liberties in the United States. The CNSS is the only nonprofit human rights and civil liberties organization whose core mission is to prevent claims of national security from eroding civil liberties or constitutional procedures. Its Web site contains articles dealing with all aspects of this issue.

Electronic Frontier Foundation (EFF)
454 Shotwell St., San Francisco, CA   94110
415-436-9333 • fax: 415-436-9993
e-mail: information@eff.org
Web site: www.eff.org

Electronic Frontier Foundation is a nonprofit organization whose mission is to defend free speech, privacy, innovation, and consumer rights. The EFF works primarily by bringing and defending lawsuits and by mobilizing citizens to lobby against undesirable legislation. Its Web site contains legal documents plus other information for the public, including the details of its class action suit against AT&T for involvement in the NSA domestic spying program and links to video interviews with whistleblower Mark Klein.

Electronic Privacy Information Center (EPIC)
1718 Connecticut Ave. NW, Suite 200
Washington, DC   20009
202-483-1140 • fax: 202-483-1248
Web site: www.epic.org

The Electronic Privacy Information Center is a public interest research center in Washington, D.C. EPIC was established in 1994 to focus public attention on emerging civil liberties issues and to protect privacy, First Amendment rights, and other constitutional laws. It publishes the *EPIC Alert*, an award-winning e-mail and online newsletter on civil liberties in the information age, and back issues are available at its

Web site. EPIC also publishes reports and books about privacy, open government, free speech, and other important topics related to civil liberties.

Liberty Coalition
e-mail: mostrolenk@libertycoalition.net
Web site: www.libertycoalition.net

The Liberty Coalition works to organize, support, and coordinate transpartisan public policy activities related to civil liberties and basic human rights. It works in conjunction with groups of partner organizations that are interested in preserving the Bill of Rights, personal autonomy, and individual privacy. It publishes an electronic newsletter that is archived at its Web site.

People for the American Way
2000 M St. NW, Suite 400, Washington, DC 20036
202-467-4999
e-mail: pfaw@pfaw.org
Web site: www.pfaw.org

People for the American Way is a nonprofit educational organization that is engaged in lobbying and other forms of political activism. Its purpose is to affirm "the American Way," by which it means pluralism; individuality; freedom of thought, expression, and religion; a sense of community; and tolerance and compassion for others. Its Web site contains press releases about recent and upcoming cases involving constitutional rights, including those related to domestic surveillance.

Preserving Life and Liberty
U.S. Department of Justice, 950 Pennsylvania Ave. NW
Washington, DC 20530
e-mail: AskDOJ@usdoj.gov
Web site: www.lifeandliberty.gov

Preserving Life and Liberty is a portion of the official U.S. Department of Justice Web site containing detailed information about the Protect America Act, which amended the Foreign

Intelligence Surveillance Act (FISA), and the USA Patriot Act. It includes congressional testimony and speeches as well as an explanation of these acts and their complete text.

Bibliography

Books

Mark Andrejevic	*iSpy: Surveillance and Power in the Interactive Era*. Lawrence: University Press of Kansas, 2007.
Stewart A. Baker and John Kavanagh, eds.	*Patriot Debates: Experts Debate the USA Patriot Act*. Chicago: American Bar Association, 2005.
Peter Berkowitz, ed.	*The Future of American Intelligence*. Stanford, CA: Hoover Institution Press, 2005.
Richard K. Betts	*Enemies of Intelligence: Knowledge and Power in American National Security*. New York: Columbia University Press, 2007.
Whitfield Diffie and Susan Landau	*Privacy on the Line: The Politics of Wiretapping and Encryption*. Cambridge, MA: MIT Press, 2007.
Amitai Etzioni	*How Patriotic Is the Patriot Act? Freedom Versus Security in the Age of Terrorism*. New York: Routledge, 2004.
Peter Hennessy, ed.	*The New Protective State: Government, Intelligence and Terrorism*. New York: Continuum, 2007.
David H. Holtzman	*Privacy Lost: How Technology Is Endangering Your Privacy*. San Francisco: Jossey-Bass, 2006.

Loch K. Johnson and James J. Wirtz, eds.
Intelligence and National Security: The Secret World of Spies. New York: Oxford University Press, 2007.

Patrick Radden Keefe
Chatter: Dispatches from the Secret World of Global Eavesdropping. New York: Random House, 2005.

Donald F. Kettl
System Under Stress: Homeland Security and American Politics. Washington, DC: CQ Press, 2007.

William E. Odom
Fixing Intelligence: For a More Secure America. New Haven, CT: Yale University Press, 2004.

Robert O'Harrow Jr.
No Place to Hide. New York: Free Press, 2005.

Eric A. Posner and Adrian Vermeule
Terror in the Balance: Security, Liberty, and the Courts. New York: Oxford University Press, 2007.

Richard A. Posner
Countering Terrorism: Blurred Focus, Halting Steps. Lanham, MD: Rowman & Littlefield, 2007.

Richard A. Posner
Preventing Surprise Attacks: Intelligence Reform in the Wake of 9/11. Lanham, MD: Rowman & Littlefield, 2005.

Richard A. Posner
Remaking Domestic Intelligence. Stanford, CA: Hoover Institution Press, 2005.

Richard A. Posner   *Uncertain Shield: The U.S. Intelligence System in the Throes of Reform.* Lanham, MD: Rowman & Littlefield, 2006.

Thomas Powers   *Intelligence Wars: American Secret History from Hitler to Al-Qaeda.* New York: New York Review Books, 2004.

Thomas Quiggin   *Seeing the Invisible: National Security Intelligence in an Uncertain Age.* Hackensack, NJ: World Scientific, 2007.

Jeffrey T. Richelson   *The U.S. Intelligence Community.* Boulder, CO: Westview Press, 2008.

James Risen   *State of War: The Secret History of the CIA and the Bush Administration.* New York: Free Press, 2006.

Jennifer E. Sims and Burton L. Gerber, eds.   *Transforming U.S. Intelligence.* Washington, DC: Georgetown University Press, 2005.

Athan Theoharis   *The Quest for Absolute Security: The Failed Relations Among U.S. Intelligence Agencies.* Chicago: Ivan R. Dee, 2007.

Amy B. Zegart   *Spying Blind: The CIA, the FBI, and the Origins of 9/11.* Princeton, NJ: Princeton University Press, 2007.

Periodicals

Tresa Baldas	"Feds' Cell Phone Tracking Divides the Courts," *National Law Journal*, January 19, 2006.
Jane Black	"More Spy Powers for the FBI? Bad Move," *Business Week Online*, March 18, 2004.
Brian Braiker	"Wiretapping the Web," *Newsweek*, August 13, 2004.
Marcia Clemmitt	"Privacy in Peril: The Issues," *CQ Researcher*, November 17, 2006.
Luke E. Debevec	"Debating the Merits of the Recent Wiretapping Decision," *Legal Intelligencer*, August 24, 2006.
Economist	"Learning to live with Big Brother," September 29, 2007.
Thomas R. Eddlem	"The Surveillance State Unveiled," *New American*, June 26, 2006.
Rudolph W. Giuliani	"Taking Liberties with the Nation's Security," *New York Times*, December 17, 2005.
Michael Isikoff et al.	"Bush's Bad Connection," *Newsweek*, February 20, 2006.
Susan Landau	"Security, Wiretapping, and the Internet," *IEEE Security & Privacy*, November–December 2005.

Eric Lichtblau and Carl Hulse — "Democrats Seem Ready to Extend Wiretap Powers," *New York Times*, October 9, 2007.

Eric Lichtblau and James Risen — "Defense Lawyers in Terror Cases Plan Challenges Over Spy Efforts," *New York Times*, December 28, 2005.

Eric Lichtblau and James Risen — "Spy Agency Mined Vast Data Trove, Officials Report," *New York Times*, December 24, 2005.

Andrew C. McCarthy — "The ACLU Loses in Court," *Weekly Standard*, July 23, 2007.

Andrew C. McCarthy — "The Patriot Act Without Tears," *National Review*, June 14, 2004.

Peter Monaghan — "The Watchers," *Chronicle of Higher Education*, March 17, 2006.

Richard A. Posner — "Wire Trap—What if Wiretapping Works?" *New Republic*, February 6, 2006.

James Risen — "Bush Signs Law to Widen Reach for Wiretapping," *New York Times*, August 6, 2007.

James Risen and Eric Lichtblau — "Bush Lets U.S. Spy on Callers Without Courts," *New York Times*, December 16, 2005.

James Risen and Eric Lichtblau — "Spying Program Snared U.S. Calls," *New York Times*, December 21, 2005.

Matthew Rothschild — "King George," *Progressive*, February 1, 2006.

Julian Sanchez   "Inside the Puzzle Palace," *Reason*,
                         April 1, 2006.

Richard Henry   "The Patriot Act and the Wall Be-
Seamon and   tween Foreign Intelligence and Law
William Dylan   Enforcement," *Harvard Journal of
Gardner   Law & Public Policy*, Spring 2005.

Patricia Smith   "Is the Government Listening?" *New
                         York Times Upfront*, February 20,
                         2006.

David Stout   "Federal Judge Orders End to War-
                         rantless Wiretapping," *New York
                         Times*, August 17, 2006.

Joelle Tessler   "Privacy Battle Shaping Up Over Cell
                         Phone Tracking," *CQ Weekly*, June
                         26, 2006.

Karen Tumulty   "Inside Bush's Secret Spy Net," *Time*,
                         May 22, 2006.

Mortimer B.   "Let's Use All the Tools," *U.S. News
Zuckerman   & World Report*, May 29, 2006.

Index

A

Accountability, of president, 115–116

Algorithms, for detecting criminal activity, 223

American Civil Liberties Union (ACLU), 143, 172

Anonymity, 15

Ascertainment requirement, 70, 83

Ashcroft, John, 67

Authorization for Use of Military Force (AUMF), 92–93, 118–119, 125–126, 130–131

B

Bankston, Kevin S., 181

Barr, Bob, 63

Battle, Jeffrey Leon, 53–57, 59–60

Benziadi, Sofiane, 56

Bjarnason, Jared, 38–39

Brandeis, Louis, 121

Breach of contract suits, against telecom companies, 16–17

Bryan, Charles, 58

Buchanan, Mary Beth, 47

Burden of proof, 74–75

Bush administration

    abuses of, 182

    defense of NSA wiretapping program by, 90, 105–106, 116–117, 129

Bush, George W.

    FISA modernization proposals by, 165–166

    on homeland security, 23–25

    on immunity for telecom companies, 17

    NSA wiretapping and, 87, 113–122

    on PATRIOT Act, 22–30

    support for Protect America Act by, 141–144

    on war on terror, 22–23

C

Call content, 206

Call details, 206

Cameron, Scott, 214

Carter, Jimmy, 112

Cell phone tracking, 214–218

Center for Democracy and Technology (CDT), 193

Circuit-switched technology, 207–208

Civil liberties

    NSA wiretapping and, 94–95, 136–139

    PATRIOT Act does not violate, 36–37

    PATRIOT Act protects, 29–30, 39–40

Clarke, Richard, 138

Clinton, Bill, 108–109

Cole, David, 129

Communications Assistance for Law Enforcement Act (CALEA)

    cell phone tracking and, 216–217

    ISPs and, 194

    modernizes wiretapping, 204–209

    passage of, 203

    VoIP and, 194, 211–213

Computer crimes, 44